For Julian Zahim

With every kind wish

Sidney Brown

Dec. 1987

NO TIME FOR TEARS

Childhood in a Rabbi's Family

No Time for Tears

Childhood in a Rabbi's Family

SIDNEY BLOCH

WILLIAM KIMBER · LONDON

First published in 1980 by
WILLIAM KIMBER & CO. LIMITED
Godolphin House, 22a Queen Anne's Gate,
London, SW1H 9AE

© Sidney Bloch, 1980
ISBN 0 7183 0497 7

This book is copyright. No part of it may be reproduced in any form without permission in writing from the publishers except by a reviewer who wishes to quote brief passages in connection with a review written for inclusion in a newspaper, magazine, radio or television broadcast.

Typeset by Granada Typesetting
and printed and bound in Great Britain by
Redwood Burn Limited, Trowbridge and Esher

*IN MEMORY
OF
MY MOTHER*

Contents

	Preface	9
I	About One Decade	11
II	The Long Stop	32
III	The Seventh Day	38
IV	Applied Chemistry	56
V	Thinking Poor	60
VI	Timothy	65
VII	The Tea Party	71
VIII	Jubilee Day	77
IX	The Code	84
X	Rachel	88
XI	Days of Challenge	92
XII	One Man Alone	110
XIII	Beyond The Fringe	114
XIV	Lost Chord	118
XV	The Munich Crisis	123
XVI	Loose Connection	127
XVII	My Uncle Harry	133
XVIII	Apprenticeship	138
XIX	Happy Birthday	172

Preface

A large black cloud fell suddenly across the mountain slopes of La Plagne as it was struck by an unexpected snowstorm. Unaccountably, I had followed an unfamiliar ski run and with visibility reduced to a few feet within a matter of seconds, I realized that I was lost. It was quite impossible to consider skiing farther and I felt distinctly uneasy when my repeated calls brought no answer. But I was extremely fortunate.

As I peered into the distance, I recognized the outline of a small hut which was close to a disused ski-lift. A few moments later I had removed my skis and taken them into the hut. It was completely bare but for a stretcher and two blankets. There was only one other occupant, a tall man in his early fifties, who helped with my skis when I entered and then immediately offered me a swig from his brandy flask. He introduced himself as Jack Jessurin, a Dutchman on holiday, who had also lost his way on the ski slopes.

We sat down on the wooden floor and he generously shared the rest of his brandy with me. Fortunately, like many Dutch people, he spoke remarkably good English. We spent the next three hours exchanging personal thoughts, fears and stories of our past. As the biting wind lashed the fresh snow to the hut, I found myself telling this complete stranger incidents which involved my parents, my three brothers and two sisters and the people who had been an influence on my life.

Preface

Spelling out the details without embarrassment or hesitation emphasized the close ties which had bound members of my family over the years and the rather special relationship which I shared with my brother Maurice in our childhood.

When the cloud eventually lifted, we were able to force the door open against the snow and prepare to finish our long ski run. At that moment, Jack Jessurin challenged me to write an account of my early years. What now follows is my acceptance, intended as a record of those who made the memories.

SIDNEY BLOCH
March, 1980

I

About One Decade

The year 1889 was probably one of the most momentous in the latter part of the nineteenth century. In England the workers were excited by the great London dock strike and the formation of the Gasworkers Union. The Tory press were convinced that any increase in tax would dilute the British way of life and Sir James Barrie published a selection of sketches of Scottish village life. In the USA, Washington and North and South Dakota were admitted states in the Union and Mark Twain produced another novel. As the year progressed the French Revolutionary Party held a provocative meeting in Bordeaux and a man named Alexandre Gustav Eiffel built a tower in Paris that was 984 feet high. It was a great year for the French because Toulouse-Lautrec shocked his family with another bawdy painting when the French art world was busily promoting Renoir.

The international press had barely reported the abdication of King Milan of Serbia when the Russian aristocrats changed their legal system and swore allegiance to a military government. This innovation had a very disturbing effect on millions of people, but did not discourage Tchaikovsky from writing *The Sleeping Princess* in the same year. Still, Germany was going through one of its more civilized periods and Chancellor Bismarck created history by introducing an old age pension insurance scheme.

It was certainly a good year for printer's ink; newspapers

were rolling off the presses at a rate of knots. Chicago built its first skyscraper, a man called Eastman produced photographic film, Cézanne painted 'Harlequin', the Crown Prince of Austria committed suicide and America declared a public holiday to celebrate one hundred years since George Washington was elected President. Most of the world's rich believed in their divine right to stay so and the poor were encouraged to thank God for their lot.

It was perhaps not surprising that, beyond a ten-mile radius, few people heard that the Lithuanian town of Krottingen was practically destroyed by fire. Most of the inhabitants lost their entire possessions because fire-fighting equipment, in that period, was entirely limited to small water-buckets and long prayers. Neither proved effective and the convent where the blaze started was destroyed together with most of the churches and synagogues in the town. In perspective, the damage and distress which the fire brought to this Baltic seaport were more severe than that suffered by London two hundred and twenty-three years earlier. Tragedy stalked the threshold of every family, but the inhabitants of the nearby towns considered themselves too poor to offer much assistance.

It was indeed a fortunate coincidence that in the same year, 1889, a young Krottingen rabbi named Isaac S. Bloch should receive a call from the Jewish community of Sunderland to become their spiritual leader. Although his Talmudic scholarship was already well-known to this Anglo-Jewish congregation, his reputation was enhanced by the ten generations of rabbinical leaders in Krottingen from whom he was directly descended. Taking his young wife and two children and their meagre possessions, he boarded a Ukrainian cargo boat that was carrying a shipment of wheat to England. The Sunderland community received him with the warmth and respect which the well-bred afford to the scholar. His outstanding Biblical knowledge was revered even though it had been barely tempered with any secular education. The rabbi settled well in northern England where his community grew and his wife gave him three more children. His sons, Harry and George, attended the local grammar schools where they excelled in their studies. Their religious education was catered for by their father who endeavoured to help them achieve a standard befitting their ancestry. Known for his deep piety and wisdom, the old man lacked the sense of humour which was subsequently developed by both his sons. Rabbi Bloch died before I was born, but his son George was my father.

*

During the early years of the twentieth century the privileged few in Russia owned immeasurable fortunes and estates whilst millions of uneducated peasants died of starvation. Leon Trotsky established a blood-bath in St Petersburg, and the Government were desperate for scapegoats as they fanned the flames of hate across their continent. Life was cheap, food was scarce and an ideal stage was set for a long series of massacres of defenceless Jews. Having concentrated on scholarship and industry, the leading members of many Jewish communities created jealousy by accepting the responsibility of adequately looking after their own poor. It was understandable that many of these hounded people should try to escape to countries which they believed to be more civilized. Several thousand travelled on the decks of tiny boats into British ports and were welcomed by their co-religionists who were already established. In those early years, very few were able to make an adequate livelihood and, in the poor economic climate in England, large numbers of refugees became dependent on their fellow-Jews.

The plight of all these foreign Jews in distress made a deep impact on one of England's foremost bankers, Samuel Montagu, the first Baron Swaythling. An orthodox Jew who was regularly consulted by a succession of Chancellors of the Exchequer, he assumed the leadership of this large number of poor immigrants. Many owed their lives to his generosity, as well as the success which their children won in the fields of science, commerce and industry. During the first decade of the century many communal centres and synagogues were established by these families in the East End of London. They were led by dedicated men of learning and humility and slowly began to adapt to their new environment. It was indeed a daunting task for an Anglo-Jewish member of the British Establishment to head a conglomeration of several dozen small foreign communities. It became increasingly apparent to Lord Swaythling that this Federation of Synagogues desperately needed a new type of leader. A history of the period records his lordship's declaration that he was looking for 'an intellectual gentleman with the highest rabbinical qualifications coupled with a university background. In addition to being a scholar, the man must be a first-class preacher, have the ability to mix freely at all levels in Anglo-Jewish society, and be prepared to devote himself to the welfare of working-class Jews.'

There was no one in England who met these requirements and pressure was put on Lord Swaythling to appoint one or other of the many applicants for the job. However the Montagus had not built their reputation by admitting defeat so readily, and his lordship left England with a mission: to find the man he had described. Travelling from one continental community to another, he found great men with learning but without wisdom, Talmudical scholars with no secular knowledge, great preachers who lacked humility, dedicated rabbis without adequate experience.

At the end of a two-year search, Samuel Montagu had not met the man he wanted, but he had repeatedly heard the name of one outstanding Hungarian rabbi who had distinguished himself in every field of philosophical and rabbinical scholarship. He was an impressive-looking family man of fifty years of age who was guided by his conscience, influenced by his vast knowledge and motivated by the needs of his fellow-Jews and other souls in distress. He was a man who, in his generation, carried a torch for Judaism and a dream for humanity. His name was Rabbi Dr M. Jung, and there are many in England today who can be grateful to Lord Swaythling for having persuaded this outstanding spiritual leader to minister to the Federation of Synagogues. He arrived in this country in 1911 and died in 1921. I never knew him, but his eldest daughter, Lolla, was my mother, and my brother Maurice is named after him.

My parents married in 1915 on the same day as Nurse Edith Cavell was executed by the Germans. Father already had his rabbinical degree, but had elected to join his brother in business. It was not unusual, in those days, for the sons of eminent rabbis to be ordained before deciding on their ultimate careers. The practice ensured that most orthodox communities would include in their membership a number of learned laymen. The commercial exercise progressed remarkably well for a while, but it was not to last. Father returned to the profession for which he had been trained and accepted the position of minister to a small community in north London.

By the end of the First World War, my eldest sister, Esther, and my brother, Sonnie, were joined by a third child, Romie. Materially, life was far from easy for the family, but my parents were ever-conscious that numerous war-stricken homes were having an even harder time. The enormous demands made on a conscientious minister allowed Father little time to spend with his young family. Despite all the difficulties, my parents stumbled through their outstanding bills with an abounding faith which was rarely shared by their bank manager. It was not customary for orthodox Jewish couples to discuss family planning, regardless of their financial circumstances. No doubt this partly accounted for my arrival in 1924, only eighteen months before Maurice joined the family.

At that time we lived in the top half of a large old house in north London. The accommodation was far from adequate, so a great deal of our time was spent in the local park. My recollections of those early years are vague as I was under five years old when we moved to Ilford in Essex. I do recall that we laughed a great deal and that we were frequently visited by relations who enjoyed singing. In my mind's eye I can still see large plates of soup filled with pieces of bread, and I can never remember my mother complaining.

During the next few years Father's financial position did not improve at all and it was a feat of the imagination to think how my mother coped with the young family. Her remarkable achievement was not helped by the arrival of the two youngest members of the family, Judith and Leonard. They appeared at twenty-month intervals and provided our parents with even more daunting and absorbing challenges. A large, untidy lady, known as Mrs Ruby, would often arrive, without warning, to give Mother a helping hand for a few hours. She charged only a pittance, but in many ways it was difficult to appreciate how she coped with so much work. In later years Mother claimed that Mrs Ruby could make a cabbage go further than anyone she knew. She was an untrained seasoning expert and, apart from giving potato soup a flavour of cabbage, she managed to give the cabbage a very distinct flavour of meat for the main course. This was her real secret as the meat itself was almost non-existent. Unfortunately, the good lady had two major problems: she only seemed able to cook cabbage-orientated dishes and she spoke to herself incessantly. Invariably her conversation would centre around her absentee husband whose surname she never disclosed.

'Wait till I see Ruby, may I never wish him harm,' she would mumble, and at this point she would inhale deeply and then quietly pour out her aspirations. 'I'll kill him!' This would be followed by her right hand bringing down the chopper smartly across a piece of cabbage. 'Ruby, my old darling,' she would sniff, 'you don't know what's coming to you,' and the chopper would repeat its performance. I'm sure that Mother was grateful for her help because she was cheap, she could stretch a cabbage a long way and she was kind to the children.

Life was fairly predictable, but never boring. Unfortunately, many outside pressures prevented our father from giving us as much of his time as we would have liked. He was a man who enjoyed relating amusing anecdotes until tears rolled down his face and we were happy when time enabled him to share his memories with us. Stories of the First World War were among our favourites, and though he spoke little about himself controlling stretcher-bearing parties, he was happy to relate tales about his cousins.

Some of my earliest recollections are of the family sitting round a bright fire which also served to light the room on a Saturday afternoon. The friendly chatter would suddenly break into a sing-song and Father would hold the floor with a big happy smile on his face. After a while the singing would stop and Father would invariably start his tales with the story of the Mayor and Aldermen of Tredegar who had stood on the little railway station together with the band of the Welsh Pipers. They had assembled to welcome the first batch of survivors arriving home from the battlefields of the Western Front. Hundreds of men, women and children waved flags and cheered when the train eventually arrived at the platform. Tears poured down the cheeks of parents and sweethearts as the soldiers alighted from the carriages and fell into the outstretched arms of those who had come to greet them. My father's cousin, Isaac, a private in the First Battalion of the Welch Fusiliers, was among that little batch of men who were carried shoulder-high through the streets of the town. Nobody listened to their protests as they were fêted by the Pipers and the publicans. Shopkeepers closed their shops, children ran out from the schools and even the sick rose from their beds to join the procession. Tredegar was determined to show the rest of Wales how to welcome the valiant who had returned from the fields of death. In reality, Private Isaac had just returned from Northern Ireland where his platoon had arrived in error. But for the Armistice, he would probably have been court martialled instead of honoured in a Welsh village. Such are the fortunes of war. I remember my father telling us about the service of thanksgiving which his Uncle George had arranged when his older son had allegedly returned from battle. This branch of the family also conformed with the practices of their forebears and thanked the Almighty for sending Isaac back unharmed from the ravages of war. There was no mention of Belfast.

A similar ceremony took place when Uncle George's second son, Arnold, returned from France. He certainly had seen the Front and had an enemy helmet to prove it, but by the time he had arrived there, the Germans had surrendered. Unfortunately, poor administration delayed his homecoming, and when he eventually reached England he arrived to swell the ranks of the unemployed rather than those of the heroes. But he was fit and cheerful and the Almighty came in for his full share of thanks with the appropriate quotations from all sections of the Good Book. The fact that Arnold had to emigrate to find a job did not diminish his gratitude.

My father had another cousin, Janus, named after his grandfather, who served on the Somme and in the Dardanelles. He was a very tall and impressive-looking man who had read history at Glasgow University where he supported himself by exercising the horses from a local stable. He had a realistic and philosophical approach to life; and reckoned that whilst an officer had the same chance of being killed as a private, he at least enjoyed a better life while he was alive. Janus changed his first name to Henri, enlisted in the London Rifle Brigade and, claiming relationship to a French Count rather than a Scottish rabbi, was duly commissioned as a lieutenant. Recognizing the limited opportunity for promotion he transferred to the cavalry, where he quickly rose to the rank of major, following serious losses in France. He always claimed that more cavalrymen died from wounded horses falling on them than from German bullets, and became an expert at jumping from injured horses before they hit the ground.

Janus — or Henri — returned to England completely disillusioned with any form of religion and, after a somewhat traumatic reunion with his family, re-enlisted in the cavalry regiment as a regular army officer. He served in India with some distinction and, on the pretext of learning a foreign language, he enjoyed a long and happy relationship with an attractive German school teacher. As a result he became fluent in the language, was transferred to British Intelligence and dropped into enemy territory during the Second World War. He was one of the few who survived, undercover, until the Allies arrived and he was appropriately decorated. When he retired he moved to California, where he was instrumental in establishing a small synagogue.

Janus's decision to become a regular soldier after the First World War was a shock to his orthodox parents and caused even more distress than his having deliberately discarded his grandfather's name. On his insistence, there had been no thanksgiving service, which meant that his family did not have the little glory to which they felt entitled and the Almighty was deprived of another vote of thanks. However, he became a legend in his lifetime and all the younger members of the family adored him, even though few had actually met him. He was certainly the most romantic member of the family to serve in the First World War; a war, which, according to the law of averages, he had no right to survive.

During the next ten years Britain entered a recession, capitalism came under serious attack and my parents produced the last five of their seven children. The three facts are not related, except that it was a challenging period in which to have a large family.

No Time for Tears

There is no doubt that my mother considered each new child was a blessing and my father acknowledged it was a miracle that he could feed another hungry mouth. After every confinement my parents recited a special prayer in the synagogue, thanking God for another safe delivery. Exactly how the doctor was recognized in the partnership was never clear, but it was obvious that our parents found no conflict of loyalties. Whether you were poor or broke made no difference to Doctor Smullion or the attention he gave. Rich patients were not over-evident in the neighbourhood and those that were tended to have small families and stay healthy. If there had been a Society for Saints on Earth, Dr Smullion would have been an honoured member. Even if he was not religious, my mother treated him as though he was licensed to practise by the Almighty himself and numbered him among the righteous agnostics.

'Is there a special place in heaven for doctors?' my brother Romie once asked. He was a few years older than myself and probably the best-looking member of the family, and the most considerate when we were little.

'There is a special place for everybody who is good,' was the answer that we all found acceptable.

There is no doubt that whilst my mother was convinced that it was the will of God that she should have a large family, it was my eldest sister, Esther, who helped her cope with it. We were extremely fortunate that for many years she identified responsibility with privilege and devoted most of her leisure time to us. 'There will be a special place for you in heaven,' Romie told her one day, but I doubt very much that these words brought her the comfort that was intended.

Unfortunately, he suffered with illnesses which, in those days, were frequently confused with minor complaints, and he was often confined to his bed. There he would sit, propped up with countless pillows, with a smile on his face, listening to a radio set through a pair of earphones. One day, he suddenly yelled for the family.

'The radio says New York has crashed!' he announced in a tone of shock. 'People are rushing for shelter and everything has fallen through the floor,' he repeated several times. It was quite apparent that he had identified the crash with some type of earthquake and was very upset about the reporter's reference to the many casualties.

In reality, we were not directly affected by the great Stock Exchange disaster, as I do not believe we knew anyone who owned a share. More significantly, our level of speculation was influenced by the family consumption of bread and milk. It did not require enormous calculations; it simply monitored the number of times a week we ate meat.

The main source of entertainment for Romie was the radio, but it was obvious that constant reference to 'Companies in ruins, thousands destitute and no signs of recovery' had a very depressing effect upon him, largely because he did not understand the terminology. My parents soon realized that having the company of his tiny brother brought him considerable pleasure and Leonard became his constant companion.

It was about this time, when Leonard had just learned to speak, that he inquired: 'Do you only call the doctor when God isn't in?' He was a cute little boy with a small round face and curly fair hair. One may be spoilt when one is the youngest, but one is never allowed to forget one's position in the family hierarchy.

'Is it your fault that I haven't any younger brothers and sisters?' he asked his mother innocently. This did not exactly give her a complex, but some of us thought she felt Leonard was the wrong one to be the youngest. We suspected that had she been really concerned, she would have solved the problem. In the event, Maurice and I endeavoured to sell Leonard the idea that if he looked older, no one would believe he was the youngest. To this end, we encouraged him to rub margarine on his upper lip to produce a moustache, and part his hair in the middle. He was disappointed with the progress, so we taught him how to walk with a springy step, so that people would think he was taller. The effect caused considerable amusement, but did little for our relationship. 'If you were my son, I'd be ashamed of you,' he once said to Maurice, and that put us both in our places for some time.

The already difficult economic times were still deteriorating when my father received a call from America to consider a rabbinical position near Cleveland. Emotionally, his deep feeling of patriotism made the flattering invitation unattractive. His family had arrived from Lithuania at the turn of the century and had found refuge and contentment in a country they were proud to serve. He considered his English education an asset he wanted to pass on to his children intact as part of their heritage. But his dreams of idealism were punctuated by the thought of exchanging our very meagre life-style for one of comparative comfort. With a heavy heart, Father left his wife and seven children to visit the small community several thousand miles away. It was the year when a major earthquake hit Greece, Cousin Janus's brother Ben eloped with a married woman and my sister Esther passed her scholarship to a grammar school.

'Everything happens when Father goes away,' Romie said. My mother was shattered that the news of the 'family disgrace' had reached the children and was convinced that Cousin Ben had permanently blotted his celestial copybook. Shortly afterwards we heard that Lindbergh had flown the Atlantic, but Mother was still too upset to be impressed. Her concern for the ethical standards of the family was temporarily interrupted by the worsening of Romie's health. We had been obliged to leave Dr Smullion behind when we moved to Ilford, in Essex, and the new doctor felt that illnesses that did not get better by themselves were cured by rest and aspirin. With this approach to medicine, he failed to diagnose the fresh symptoms that Romie was developing.

'Are all doctors good?' Romie had asked with a sixth sense

that nobody recognized at the time. It was a difficult question to answer and its implication escaped all but one person. With Father miles away, a jolly doctor who used his stethoscope sparingly and no money for second opinions, my mother looked towards Heaven for help and prayed for Romie's recovery.

A lot of people were praying at that time. Thousands of disabled ex-Servicemen were walking the streets looking for work and the unemployment figures were still rising. Two of my mother's brothers, Leo and Max, graduated at Cambridge only to discover that a PhD was a qualification for the dole queue. They both emigrated to America, one to become the Professor of Comparative Religion at Columbia University and the other a prominent rabbi in New York. They were truly the intellectuals in the family and were missed long after they left.

Ramsay MacDonald was elected Prime Minister for the second time on the day a small American boat brought Father back to England. The little community that had been impressed by his scholarship and captured by his sense of humour had made him a very attractive offer. Father always said that he was determined to accept it right up to the time that he saw the white cliffs of Dover. That, to him, was the moment of truth and he knew that somehow he would struggle through and finish his days in England.

'Is God English?' Maurice asked at that time. Father looked distinctly uncomfortable. I believe he would have given his right arm to be told that his Jewish God had a British background. Obviously, he could hardly have reconciled this with his firm belief in the Scriptures. 'God understands English,' Romie offered and the answer satisfied our young brother and appeared to please Father.

Soon after he returned from America, he accepted a new appointment in Ilford, Essex, with a slightly better salary. The additional income was immediately earmarked for specialist medical attention for Romie and hope was reborn, for his early recovery. At last we were in a position to pay a consultant who understood Romie's condition. Two days after this senior physician visited our home, Romie was taken to hospital and Father went to the synagogue to pray. Hours later he sat in a restaurant, stirring a glass of hot lemon tea until it went cold. He left it, untasted, and slowly walked towards home. Almost unconsciously, he bought an evening paper and stared horrified at the picture of thousands of emaciated Indian children praying for food. Years later he claimed the picture still haunted him.

The following Friday, the telephone rang just after my mother had lit the candles. My father inhaled deeply and left the room without any comment. It was the first and only time I had known him answer the phone on the Sabbath. It was a short call from the hospital which told him that Romie had just died. There were no recriminations. No one mentioned the doctors. No one questioned God.

It had not been a good year for prayers. It was additionally distressing that Romie should have passed away only two weeks before Sonnie's Barmitzvah. This significant date in the life of my eldest brother was not allowed to pass without a religious ceremony, but there was no question of a celebration. Regardless of the timing, a reception would have been of modest proportions, but the sad circumstances made it impossible for any social event to be considered. Sonnie had an extremely pleasant voice and his rendering of the portion of the Law in the synagogue brought pleasure to all those who heard him. There were no special guests for lunch on that Saturday, but Mother did bake a cake for the occasion. Little did we realize then, that for a variety of reasons, none of the brothers in our family was destined to have anything resembling a party on the occasion of his Barmitzvah.

Accepting tragedy as part of the Divine pattern enabled our parents to cope with the loss of a child better than most. Mother had her hands full with the family and Father had a new community to think about.

'How did Romie get to the next world?' Maurice asked Father one evening.

'God arranged it,' Father said with the confidence of a man who obtains his information direct from the source. The tone of his voice discouraged further discussion on this delicate subject. It was difficult for us to appreciate the methods of transport employed by the Almighty, but if Father was satisfied, it was good enough for us.

The only event of any consequence that summer was the news that a cousin of Father's had turned up in Montreal. He had been upset when his own father had remarried and decided to leave home. We children were excited to learn that he had jumped a small cargo ship at London docks and worked his passage for six weeks to New York. There he convinced the immigration authorities that he was on a religious mission and spent several months wandering round North America looking for a permanent job. His arrival in Canada brought little comfort to his worried father, who had long believed that his prodigal son had met with a fatal accident. But news had provided the old man with reason to acknowledge publicly Divine intervention in securing the deliverance of his son. Nevertheless, he remained convinced that he had come under the influence of every heathen between north London and Montreal. In reality he settled down extremely well. Not long after his arrival in Canada he married a very charming Jewish girl and established himself in the retail trade. He became a highly respected member of the local community and was well known for his generosity to those in need.

That year, like most years, school holidays were spent at home, and the local open-air swimming pool, in Cranbrook Park, proved an excellent substitute for the seaside. It was more than adequate as I was obsessed with training for the twenty-five yards swimming competition between the schools in the borough. This involved practising daily for weeks and Maurice would join me to time my speeds. As neither of us had a watch, he perfected a system of foot-tapping that was amazingly accurate. On my bad days, I always suspected that he tapped a little slower than usual to help keep my spirits high. When the big day arrived, I came second in my heat and nowhere in the finals. It was certainly a disappointment, but remaining in the school team was a great consolation.

'It is nothing to do with your height,' Maurice said, knowing that, at that time, we both wanted to be tall like Sonnie.

'I didn't mind losing,' I lied. 'I'll get a place next time.'

'I'll bet on that,' was his encouraging reply, but neither of us wanted to discuss the stakes.

The long, dry summer created ideal courting conditions and no doubt contributed to many matrimonial commitments. Unfortunately, the numerous beneficiaries in this category did not include our unmarried young daily, Theresa. Misplaced confidence and a generous disposition towards lechery inspired her to underestimate the benefits of clergy. When our doctor had confirmed her worst fears, she rushed to her priest for words of comfort and guidance. On learning that the gates of the Kingdom of Heaven were now closed to her for ever, she decided to look to the river for her solution. Fortunately, common sense persuaded her to have lunch first, but her obvious distress soon disclosed her secret.

'Illegitimate. . . .' we overheard Father say distinctly, when Mother broke the news that she was inviting Theresa to lodge with us for a while. We did not wait for the rest of the conversation, but rushed off to find the family dictionary. The word Father had used sounded most significant, if not sinister. In the event, it was simply defined, 'born outside wedlock'. The following day, after school, we visited the library to consult a large map of England. We were more than surprised that we were quite unable to find Wedlock on the map. When we innocently mentioned this at dinner, that evening, the older members of the family broke into hysterical laughter. Tears rolled down Father's face as he laughed for the first time since Romie had died. Theresa stayed with us until Mother had been in touch with her parents and arranged for her return home to Ireland.

Slowly, the house settled down to a form of disorganized routine. Father spent most of his time coping with the problems of his own congregants and anyone else who sought his advice. His days were spent visiting the sick, the poor and the lonely, writing speeches and sermons and, when time permitted, studying various aspects of Jewish law or English literature. He was over forty when he decided to read for an honours degree in the latter.

His methods of dealing with the problems of others were often unusual, but always practical. Although he frequently had to help people to live with adversity he discouraged them from accepting defeat too readily. This was well illustrated by his reaction to an elderly shopkeeper who complained, tearfully, that he was unable to obtain a new lease. This man, Joe Lewis, had no children, but he and his wife had spent all their married life building up a first-class small business from a semi-derelict property. Allegedly, the landlord had decided that he could exploit the goodwill of the shop for the benefit of his new son-in-law. Legally the landlord was completely within his rights and owed no obligation to his tenant. The long-term distress that Joe Lewis could suffer was quite evident and Father considered the time was right for action and not for sympathy. He immediately visited the landlord who adamantly defended his attitude.

'It's business, Reverend, and it's legal,' he said. The man was absolutely right, but Father felt his job was to solve a human problem and not to enter into a debate on jurisprudence.

'Are you a good businessman?' he asked slowly. The landlord smiled and nodded confidently.

'We wouldn't be having this discussion if I wasn't,' he said. Father's brain was ticking over fast and he was making his own mathematical calculations.

'I don't think you've thought this out very carefully at all,' he started quietly and held up his hand to stop the man interrupting. 'Joe Lewis knows his business inside out. Your son-in-law has no experience or training in trade and I think he could kill the goodwill inside a year and –' he hesitated, to give his words greater emphasis – 'he will probably lose all the money you invest in it. If you want to protect your daughter, you should think of a compromise.'

'Like what?' the man answered cautiously.

Father waited a few moments before answering. 'Like halving the rent and getting Joe Lewis to give your son-in-law a job with a share of the profits. After all,' he went on, 'Joe will be an old man in a few years and you'll be able to do a decent deal with him then.'

The landlord's large face broke into an enormous smile. 'You're a clever man, Reverend,' he said.

The handling of this apparently impossible situation gave Father an extraordinary reputation as a negotiator and peacemaker. The Gentile landlord became a good friend of our family and Joe started attending the synagogue more often.

Not long after this incident a local school headmaster visited my father to discuss his concern for one of his teachers. This art master was an ardent Catholic, with a large family, who had recently won £15,000 on the football pools.

'That's more money than he's likely to earn in his life,' said the headmaster. My father was not an investment consultant and, at first, could not appreciate why anyone should wish to discuss the matter with him. Apparently, the news item had attracted the attention of a distinguished-looking gentleman who claimed to be an international art dealer. The headmaster, Dr Beaumont, was worried that the middle-aged member of his staff might be persuaded to invest in an unreliable enterprise.

'I have no connections in the art world,' my father told him honestly, 'but I can make one or two inquiries.'

That evening he telephoned a young solicitor named Leslie Paisner to inquire if there was any way of checking the reputation of the art connoisseur. Father had known the lawyer since he was a child and had no difficulty in recruiting his assistance. Within a few days we learned that the gentleman concerned was extremely well known in the art world. His reputation had been given considerable publicity when he had been sentenced to five years' imprisonment for fraud. Mr Paisner had found all the details of the particular case after speaking to a Bond Street dealer. Apparently, the man had the dignified appearance and manner of a highly respectable member of the trade and had cultivated an accent to complement his style. His practice was to visit the less experienced art dealers, in the provinces, and endeavour to sell one or two mediocre paintings. Invariably he failed to do so, but he would generously offer to leave the paintings with the dealer, free of any obligation, in case a customer should happen to like them. This magnanimous gesture was invariably appreciated as the impressive gentleman never requested that the paintings should be displayed in prominent positions.

Within a week or so an accomplice would arrive in a Rolls-Royce and casually browse round the innocent dealer's shop. Suddenly, he would stop and stare at one of the paintings and exclaim, 'My God, I've been looking for that artist's work for years.' He would then take out a magnifying glass, take the painting into the lightest place in the gallery and very carefully examine the signature. He would allow several minutes to elapse and then, staring at the dealer with an expression of amazement, would exclaim, 'It's genuine!' and make a cash offer of one thousand pounds. The poor dealer would be unable to sell it until he had spoken with his distinguished owner and would prevail upon his potential client to call back in a week's time.

'Call back!' the accomplice would shout loudly. 'I should say I'll call back, but I want your word as a gentleman that you will accept my offer.' This would be readily given by the excited dealer who was already calculating his profit. Two days later, the connoisseur would return to collect his paintings and the dealer would eagerly start negotiating to buy them.

'I'll give you five hundred pounds in cash,' would often be the opening offer. The distinguished-looking gentleman would stare at the paintings and say nothing.

'I could go to six hundred,' the gallery owner would say, afraid of losing his best deal of the year.

The owner would look at him kindly, with his head slightly tilted, and say quietly, 'I do not believe in making excessive profits from the sweat of great artists.' He would then hesitate and add, 'I would be happy to accept four hundred and hope we can do business again.' The sale would be completed and the dedicated art dealer would leave, promising to keep his eye open for work by the same artist. Neither he, his 'wealthy' accomplice or the hired Rolls would ever be seen in the district again.

Father told the story to Dr Beaumont immediately he heard it. The old headmaster was delighted to be able to warn his art teacher and wrote Father an extremely charming and appreciative letter. Some months later we learned that the lucky pools winner had felt that both men had lacked Christian charity and he invested his fortune with the confidence trickster. Leslie Paisner remained a good friend of Father's throughout his life. The poor, disillusioned art master continued teaching until he was seventy when he retired on a modest pension.

The problems of running a home for a husband and six children imposed considerable pressure on Mother. Her limited housekeeping allowance necessitated a level of budgeting which would have tested the skill of a financial acrobat. Providing a varied diet for an entire family at a cost of half a crown a meal was not a feat to be underestimated. But we were never hungry and there was always sufficient for an unexpected visitor who arrived to join our table. The attention and long hours that such a household demanded did not prevent Mother finding time to study commentaries on religious texts from the Old Testament, taking a keen interest in philately and conducting a large and quite amazing correspondence. Tidiness was certainly not her greatest virtue, but we tended to consider the numerous books and papers she left everywhere as the hallmark of her intellectual aspirations.

Apart from writing regularly to many members of the family, she corresponded with the editor of *The Times* on education for marriage; with the Cardinal Secretary of the Vatican on family relationships; with the Professor of Philosophy at Cambridge on comparative religion and a number of other academics in different parts of the world. She was to continue this lively and varied correspondence for over forty years.

There was a short time when Maurice was considered anaemic, and when our local doctor recommended a diet largely composed of raw meat, Mother decided to seek other medical advice. It was this incident which ultimately led her to part-conversion to homeopathic medicine. Suddenly, there was a great abundance of fruit, vegetables, nuts and yoghourt and a marked reduction in the consumption of meat and eggs. In general terms, the family were fairly indifferent to the change-over, but Father did not come under the new influence. He did not take kindly to radical changes and his diet remained entirely unaltered. Actuaries may well speculate whether any conclusions can be drawn from the fact that Mother outlived Father by thirty-eight years. Her new doctor, Eric Lederman, in whom she had enormous confidence, pioneered many of the cures which have today been accepted by the conservative medical profession. Maurice was cured without raw meat and Mother firmly believed that Dr Lederman made a major contribution to her long years of good health.

A year after Romie died, a black spaniel called Prince joined our family. He belonged to all of us. He was that sort of dog.

II

The Long Stop

One of the oldest cemeteries on the borders of Ilford is situated right next door to the town's swimming pool. Had this not been the case, it is doubtful if any part of the following incident would ever have been recorded.

The afternoon was not sufficiently cold to justify an overcoat but it became quite cool as the early summer sun was beginning to turn in for the night. The endless line of southbound traffic had quietly come to a halt to make way for a funeral procession turning into the gates of the cemetery. In the days of the recession, mourning was a luxury except for the unemployed. A funeral was rarely considered an adequate reason for absenteeism even if one could afford the resultant loss of pay. Few could and even fewer did make such a sacrifice, except for very close relations. Consequently, a funeral procession of two cars, including the hearse, was considered quite normal by the majority of people familiar with the economic climate and its demands. After all, at a time when work is short and money is scarce, wakes become a luxury. This philosophy was so readily accepted that few even allowed their eyes to follow the hearse as it carried its star passenger to his final resting-place.

The two young boys standing on the steps of the swimming pool building were the only obvious exceptions. With our towels under our arms, we stood and watched. First, the large, black hearse, carrying the flower-covered coffin and two gentlemen, and then the small green Ford which looked overcrowded with four weeping women.

'What a sad funeral,' said Maurice. 'So few people,' he muttered.

'Perhaps he was very old,' I offered. 'Perhaps all his family have already died.'

'It doesn't matter,' my brother insisted. 'Even if an old man dies, people can pretend they were his friends. Just for once.'

'Perhaps his friends haven't heard about it yet,' I tried again.

'Everybody hears when a friend dies. What sort of friend doesn't hear when a friend dies?' he asked knowledgeably.

We walked slowly and silently down the rest of the steps where our feet and our thoughts took us through the cemetery gates. I can well remember Maurice had one sock hanging down his leg because he had lost an elastic garter and my maroon swimming costume was sticking out of my wet towel. We waited for the mourners to come out of the Chapel and pondered on the mission we had undertaken so impulsively.

'They won't know who we are,' I said, as though we were half-expected guests.

'Don't matter,' said Maurice aggressively. 'Nobody should have only six people at his funeral. Nobody. Not even somebody who nobody knows.'

The logic of this profound statement might well have justified some clarification at a later stage, but my young brother had made his message quite clear. It was obvious to me that he was feeling the occasion very deeply, but I felt obliged, as his older brother, to counter his reasoning.

'Perhaps he was a robber?' I suggested encouragingly.

'Don't matter,' was the answer. 'If he was, he wasn't always a robber and maybe he was a nice robber anyway.'

'Perhaps he didn't want a lot of people to come,' I said, hoping it might make Maurice feel a bit better about the whole matter.

'Perhaps nobody asked him,' and he set his chin when he said it.

No Time for Tears

Our deliberations were interrupted by the sounds of opening doors and weeping women. The bier came out first, followed by the two men pushing it; then the four women in black who walked slowly, in twos, towards the open grave. Maurice and I stared hard, making the facial expressions which we felt most appropriate for the occasion. Clutching our swimming gear, we nodded our heads to one another and, without a word, joined the end of the procession.

The actual burial took only a few minutes, but we waited respectfully until all the earth had been replaced and the wreaths arranged around the grave. It is difficult to recall whether we imagined it was politeness or simply curiosity to bend down and inspect the cards attached to the various floral offerings. They were from near relatives and distant cousins and local friends and members of a working-men's club and they all carried inscriptions like, 'Deepest Sympathy to Mrs Clayton', 'You were a good friend Fred' and similar expressions which mourners throughout the world consider apposite. Then, I came across one which was different. It was written in large, round letters with the following message over many signatures: 'From all your crew mates on bus route 144, with happy memories.' Suddenly, I felt related to the man who had just been buried. He was no longer a lonely stranger with a handful of mourners. He was Fred Clayton of bus route 144, the route I took to and from school every day. I never actually knew him and I certainly could not put a face to the name, but nevertheless, I identified myself as a personal mourner.

Leaning down over the wreaths, I whispered my discovery to Maurice, who readily acknowledged the relationship by shaking his head from side to side with fresh sympathy. Slowly, I raised my head from the wreaths and was shaken to see the widow staring at me through her black veil. Her tears had stopped and she just stared and made me feel that I should either say something or run away.

I took two steps towards her, clutched my blue school-cap in my hand, and said, 'All the boys will miss him very much.'

She burst into tears, raised her veil and gave me a big wet kiss.

We barely spoke until we were nearly home, when Maurice burst out, 'You just told the loveliest lie I ever heard.'

Unfortunately, we were not to have the opportunity, that evening, of telling the story of the afternoon's experience. Far more significant incidents were to be the subjects of conversation. When we burst into the house it had just been announced on the radio that Captain Alfred Dreyfus, a retired French Jewish army officer, had died at the age of seventy-six. This news did not affect any other eleven-year-old boy that I knew, but it was quite obvious that Father thought it should affect his children.

'I remember Dreyfus being honoured, in Paris, in 1902,' Father said, as though he had been there at the time.

'What had he done?' we all asked together.

Father looked amazed when he heard the question. It was quite obvious from his expression that he expected us to be more than familiar with the story. 'He was an innocent man who spent twelve years on Devil's island.' He spoke as though we all knew the place well. 'You know,' he reminisced, 'but for a writer called Emile Zola he would have spent the rest of his life there.'

'Was Mr Zola Jewish?' Maurice asked.

'He was a great writer,' Father said, avoiding the question: 'This was a victory for justice,' he said. Father had never been nearer to Dreyfus than a photograph in *The Times* and, but for the case, could never have identified with him. Nonetheless, he still created the impression that if he ever updated the Old Testament, he would include the Dreyfus story somewhere.

'Mr Zola died before he could be honoured,' Mother informed us sadly. We did not have time to discuss this unkind stroke of fate as our conversation was interrupted by the arrival of a Mrs Lander. She was in a state of considerable distress as her husband had just been sentenced to three months' imprisonment. Without a word, we all left the room leaving our parents to listen to one of Father's congregants unfold her sad story. Apparently, Mr Lander had been a very unsuccessful dress salesman, working on commission. When the local tradesmen refused to give his wife any further credit he sold some of the firm's stock privately. It was his first offence but the magistrate felt that the punishment might well make it his only one.

'Why didn't you come before?' Father asked kindly.

'We were too ashamed,' was the answer that could have been expected. This was the only case of a member of the congregation actually going to prison during the entire time Father occupied the pulpit. It was not too difficult for Mother to muster help for this unfortunate family. Father visited Moss Lander every week and invariably took a home-made cake with him. What, perhaps, was more significant was that he also took books on salesmanship in the hope of improving Mr Lander's technique. On each occasion he would test the man on what he had learned from the last book. One of them was called *Alternative Methods of Selling Honestly* and included the following advice:

> When selling to retail shops, do not refer to bargains but to special opportunities. 'Cannot be repeated' is better than 'bankrupt stock' and 'the material is too good for the price' is preferable to 'cheap'!

When Moss Lander emerged from jail, a chastened and wiser salesman, Father found him a job. 'I've got it for you on my reputation,' he told him pointedly.

Within a short time, Moss Lander had become a very successful sales executive, and he stayed with that same firm for twenty-five years, until his retirement. Neither he nor his wife ever visited our house again and he became a member of another synagogue.

'He is entitled to his pride,' Father always said when the man was discussed. Years later we heard that one of his sons had joined the company and become a director and his other son practised as a barrister.

When we eventually told our parents about our visit to the cemetery, they appeared both amused and touched. 'Some people walk backwards away from a new grave,' Mother said, and then explained. 'It's considered a mark of respect for the person who's been buried.'

This was the first time I had heard of the custom but Maurice said, 'I walked away backwards.'

'How did you know?' Father asked.

'I didn't, he said quietly, 'I had a big hole in my sock.'

III

The Seventh Day

Holidays and Sundays had a great deal in common in our family. The mornings would be spent in some form of religious instruction and the afternoons were reserved exclusively for recreation. Our own ideas and inventions always gave us so much to do with our limited leisure time that I cannot think when we would have played with toys, had we had any.

The local park, which was only a ten-minute walk from home, probably afforded us the greatest opportunities for entertainment, pleasure and mischief. Apart from the normal games, Maurice and I would make special events out of tracking with our dog and tadpole fishing.

'I think we should take Judith,' he announced one Friday during a school holiday. The idea that he should suggest that our little sister be included in our fishing party was heretical. Firstly, she was a girl; secondly, she was small; and thirdly, she knew nothing about tadpole fishing.

'Why?' I asked. 'You know she'll be in our way,' I added lamely.

'We can't do two things properly at the same time,' was the enigmatic answer. He then creased his forehead into his favourite frown and added, 'I think catching good tadpoles is one job and holding the jam-jars is another job and Judith could hold the jam-jars.' This apparently simple suggestion was no doubt prompted by the inexplicable bad luck we had suffered as fishermen. Consistently, we had caught tadpoles that had either lost the will to live or were in the advanced stages of some terminal disease. Whichever it was, they rarely survived more than a day and Maurice's proposal was made in the belief that if we didn't have to worry about the jam-jars, we could concentrate on catching healthy tadpoles.

Judith was so thrilled at being included in the party that she dropped one of the jars on the pavement. We returned home to replace it. In order to do so, we poured the remains of a jar of marmalade into a jar of peanut butter in the hope that the eventual discovery would create amusement rather than distress. The delay brought us to the park later than usual and we were obliged to run most of the way, as the pond was some distance from the gates. There was no doubt that Judith brought us good luck, as our catch was phenomenal. Maurice was quite convinced that it was his discerning eye which spotted the healthier tadpoles and the lesson to concentrate on only one thing at a time has served him ever since. What neither of us appreciated at the time was that Judith, impatiently waiting for her brothers, had emptied the fresh water from the jars and refilled them with water from the stream. This obviously encouraged the tadpoles to make a greater effort to survive, but the principle of one man, one job, was well established for future expeditions.

Sudden realization that the afternoon was drawing to a rapid close caused us to collect our gear hurriedly. Late Friday afternoon was the time for preparing for the Sabbath and not for fishing expeditions. I do not believe that we were afraid of being late because we thought that Saturday belonged to God, but rather that we shared it with Him, and felt it unforgivable to cause offence. Apart from this theological consideration, we always changed into our best clothes to attend the synagogue service. This was conducted by Father, who was the minister of the local Jewish community. The services were not very well supported on Friday evenings and not that much better on

Saturdays, but as the synagogue was small the effect was not depressing. I can never remember Father referring to those who did not attend, but Mother felt very strongly that such people were not so much desecrating the Sabbath Day as depriving themselves of the pleasure of observing it. Our parents had no doubt whatsoever that the Almighty was always present and somehow implied that membership of the synagogue included His patronage.

It was accepted that Shabbat was reserved for prayer, study and possibly walks. Mother prepared all the meals for the Sabbath on Friday, and whilst games like chess and draughts were permitted, Monopoly was strictly forbidden. Strangely enough, although we lived and moved in a Gentile society, we did not feel any resentment that the Almighty and our parents made these demands on us every week.

'Do you think God likes football?' Maurice asked me one Saturday when we were walking back from service. I found the question amusing, but guessed that there was a reason behind it.

'Why? Have you been praying for some team to win?'

'No,' he answered and gave me a look which told me he was quite offended by my remark. He hesitated just long enough for his next words to carry additional emphasis. 'There are four of our masters in the Borough Teachers' Team and they're playing in the park this afternoon.'

The message was clear. Maurice obviously considered it reasonable that as we didn't have to travel, we should support the Masters' Team. The difficulty was getting away from our study session in time for the kick-off. After considerable discussion regarding an acceptable excuse which involved evaluating the size and implication of white lies, we agreed on our story. That afternoon we studied Ethics in relation to God and our mother told us about the 'ever-seeing eye and ever-hearing ear.' After listening to mystical stories of His spiritual computer, a boy of nine required considerable courage to tell a white lie, however white it was.

'We would like to go to the park earlier than usual today,' I suddenly announced as my mother was talking about little sins leading to bigger ones.

She did not change her expression, but simply said, 'Yes?'

'There is a free exhibition,' I said, without enlarging on it.

Before she could answer, Maurice came in well on cue: 'It's a sort of Nature Exhibition,' he offered.

To our mother, God and Nature were one, and her face broke into a smile, believing that we too acknowledged that only the Almighty was responsible for all things created.

One hour later, as we stood near one of the goal-posts, the ball came right up to us and I kicked it back to the nearest player. Maurice looked at me, and it was quite obvious that, at that time, we were both thinking about 'the seeing eye' and whether or not we were prejudicing our relationship with the Deity. Watching the match became a fortnightly event whenever the team played at home. We had little doubt that our parents knew all about the Nature Exhibition, although it was never discussed, and when the Masters' Team came top of the League, we thought God might be on our side too.

Problems concerning the observance of the Sabbath were not just restricted to children and the decisions taken sometimes had far-reaching and unexpected effect. The opening of the King George V Hospital, some three miles from our home, was scheduled to take place on a Saturday afternoon. Ministers of all denominations were invited and our parents duly received their invitation to represent the Jewish community. The occasion demanded a top hat and morning dress and, as our parents did not travel on the Sabbath, this necessitated changing at the hospital where the clothes were left on Friday. My mother nurtured some doubts as to whether it was right to attend a public function on the Sabbath. but my father made his decision without question. For reasons which we never completely understood, he always behaved as though he were directly related to the Royal Family. The religious differences were appreciated, but when Father recited the Prayer for the Royal Family in the synagogue every week, no one doubted that the Almighty was giving the petition His undivided attention.

The hospital had, of course, been functioning for several months before the official opening. This enabled the royal party and certain privileged guests to visit some of the wards and to meet members of the management and staff. Fortunately it did not rain and the open-air ceremony was performed at leisure and with dignity. Our parents were introduced to the King and Queen, but I am quite sure that my Father regretted that time and protocol did not permit an exchange of views.

'It must be marvellous for them,' I said proudly to Maurice as we walked round to the park.

He stuck his forefinger under his school-cap and scratched his head. 'It's jolly good for us too,' he laughed.

'But we're not there, are we?'

'No,' Maurice agreed, 'but we're not having lessons either.'

At that moment, a boy from our school stopped to speak to us. He had a big smile on his face and very proudly announced, 'I told my Mum and Dad your parents were meeting the King and Queen today.' Neither of us had an answer ready for him. 'I'm really glad I'm in your class,' he told me, obviously feeling that some of the glory of the occasion was rubbing off on to him. The strange part about the little incident was that I had never liked the boy until that day. Unaccountably, I was pleased he wanted to share our pleasure with us.

After the hospital ceremony, my father went back to change into his normal clothes before walking home. Suddenly, he heard his name being called. One of the nursing sisters informed him that a Jewish patient had unexpectedly become critically ill and the family wanted him urgently at the bedside. My father sat with that man for three hours until he died and his last words were, 'I knew you would be there, Reverend.'

I never heard my father relate that story a second time, but my mother was always convinced that it was providential that the opening of the King George V Hospital should have taken place on that Shabbat.

In any period, couples with six growing children, a dog and an inadequate budget, simply are not short of diverse conversation. Our parents were no exception, and the publicity given to the opening of the local hospital was the main topic of discussion for several weeks. The local newspaper reported the occasion over two pages and Father was shown in a photograph, shaking hands with the King himself. As would be expected, we were each presented with a copy, which we carried around until the individuals in the picture were quite unrecognizable. Maurice was the only one of us to appear undisturbed by this discovery.

'I've got an extra one,' he confessed quietly, one evening. Suddenly I remembered the week when he had declared a sweet-fast.

'What made you buy it?' I asked.

'I wanted a copy for my children,' he answered, as though they were living in the next street instead of twenty-five years hence.

No doubt the occasion would have retained its position of priority had it not been for a series of incidents which occurred only a few weeks later. Unexpected things began to happen one Friday afternoon when we had left school early, in order to arrive home in time for Mother to light the Sabbath candles. Friday was never just the day after Thursday or the day before Saturday. Friday was the day before Friday night. It was the highlight of our week and although the pattern remained the same, its unique novelty never wore off. Those candles signalled the commencement of a day which belonged to the Almighty and His family and that certainly included us, and was quite different from any other day in the week. There was no cooking, no travelling, no telephoning and no writing, and yet, in our childhood, we rarely felt deprived by these limitations. Even during the years of extreme economic stress, we always had better clothes reserved for the Sabbath and Festivals and less smart clothes for weekdays. The dividing line between the two was sometimes difficult to define, but it was always there. At times, the uninitiated might well have considered the difference more an attitude of mind than of sartorial reality, but we were quite unconscious of the subtleties, even when they were amusingly transparent.

'Those socks aren't good enough for the Sabbath,' I remarked to Maurice, pointing to a hole in the toe of one of his socks. There was nothing he could do about it. Mother was about to light the candles and she would never dream of darning on the Sabbath. He threw out his chin and half-closed his eyes.

'My weekday socks have *much* bigger holes in the heels,' he answered in a very dignified tone.

We had arrived home that afternoon to find a tall stranger sitting in the lounge. This was not so unusual, but he wore a long black coat and had not replaced his large black hat with the traditional skull-cap. His full grey beard made it quite impossible to guess his years, but his lively eyes and benevolent smile made his age unimportant. Mother introduced him to us, explaining that he came from Poland and spoke only Yiddish, with a strange accent. We did not understand him but gathered from Father that our guest had probably developed the accent in the belief that it made his Yiddish sound like German. During dinner he spoke only to Father, although he continually looked at Maurice and me. At no time did he address himself directly to Mother, although he made complimentary remarks concerning her cooking to everybody in general and Father in particular. He was the noisiest soup-drinker we had ever entertained and the only one who seemed completely oblivious of our expressions of amazement. By the time dinner was over both Maurice and I were quite convinced that he had been making some proposition to Father which affected us. In the kitchen Mother confided that the gentleman was recruiting students for a well-known Jewish Yeshiva on the borders of Poland.

'Nobody leaves England for Poland,' Maurice said. This was an astonishing remark, as neither of us knew where Poland was.

'What did Father say?' I asked, shaking my head with laughter.

Mother smiled for a moment and shrugging her shoulders, replied, 'He said he'd think about it.'

'He said *what*?' Maurice shouted.

'What has he got to think about?' I asked, a little too loudly.

Mother appeared amused at our worried faces. 'This man has come from the Yeshiva in Mir,' she started slowly, 'and he feels he is paying our family a great honour in offering to accept you both as students. Your Daddy,' she continued with a laugh, 'can hardly tell him how he feels about the Royal Family, but he won't offend him at his own table.'

'What does that mean?' I asked.

'It means he'll tell him after the Sabbath,' she said.

Armed with Father's large atlas we retired to our bedroom to study the various routes to and from Poland. It was a daunting exercise as neither of us had been nearer to the continent than Westcliff-on-Sea. The town of Mir was not shown on the map, but an old encyclopaedia mentioned that it was in the part of Eastern Europe inhabited by many poverty-stricken families. This piece of intelligence encouraged us to speculate on the real reasons for the stranger's visit. Maurice held his chin and shook his head. 'I don't think he's a spy,' he said, 'but he could be a slave-trader.' This incongruous idea seemed a real possibility, but there was little we could do about it.

Whatever happened, we knew the man would not travel on the Sabbath and that gave us at least a day to verify the facts. Our bedroom door did not boast a lock so Maurice jammed a chair under the handle. 'Just in case he's mad,' he said.

The following day Father confirmed that there was no question of his taking the serious proposal seriously. 'Some of the greatest Jewish scholars in the world were educated at Mir, but it's not for you two.' He spoke very seriously and only smiled when Maurice muttered, 'Thank God.'

As usual on Sunday we travelled several miles, by train, to a Yeshiva in Thrawl Street, in the heart of London's East End. The rambling building, overlooked by tenement flats, provided advanced courses of Hebrew education for all stages up to graduation. Any resemblance between this sparsely furnished Victorian establishment and a college was purely imaginary. The rooms were dark and small and the trestle tables which served as desks bore the pencil-marks of numerous restless students. It catered exclusively for the sons of those who believed that a Talmudic education provided the soundest foundation for a worthwhile lifestyle within the Jewish community. Although a number of students ultimately became rabbis, the majority of us entered the professions or commerce. Maurice and I were two of the youngest and, perhaps, most unenthusiastic boys to attend at that time.

However, our limited enthusiasm was quickly ignited by a certain Rabbi H. Meyer Bendes who was one of the kindest teachers of his generation and the most humble of men. Born in Lithuania in 1874, he was an outstanding scholar, a wonderful teacher and, at all times, a perfect gentleman. Had life treated him more kindly materially, there is no doubt that he would have been an architect of some eminence. A man blessed with a remarkable artistic talent, he accepted his humble lifestyle with a dignity that befitted his calling. Throughout my entire school life I met no teacher who was genuinely loved and respected by so many students. Those who studied with him shared a common friend and felt richer for the experience.

The modest salaries paid to the academic staff of the Thrawl Street Yeshiva would certainly have strained the dedication of less devout men.

'He looks too good for his clothes,' Maurice said one lunch-time as a duty teacher watched us eating our raisin sandwiches. This profound remark amused many of the older boys who were sitting near us and was really responsible for our getting to know them better.

'His stock is rising in heaven,' commented Harry Kingstein, who was an amusing extrovert several years our senior. Although he was an Orthodox young man, he enjoyed giving the impression of being a misplaced agnostic. One time, after all the students had been addressed on the subject of Sins and Sinners, he loudly declared his approval of Heine's quip, that God would always forgive him because it was His business to do so. Later, when I repeated this to Father, he did not appear amused. Mother, who normally disapproved even more strongly of cynical remarks, looked distinctly impressed that a young theological student could quote a German philosopher. Her religious discipline was frequently tempered by her appreciation of secular culture. (Harry changed his name to Kingston when he joined the RAF, and died when his plane was shot down over Bremen.)

A number of enthusiastic book-collectors had helped the old Yeshiva to build a large library of well-worn volumes, but the dark, ill-decorated rooms hardly appeared conducive to serious study. Despite these uninspiring surroundings, the teachers were able to imbue the students with an amazing degree of scholastic zeal. Although most of us had been press-ganged into the college, there is no doubt that the inspiration and encouragement which we received from these Talmudic teachers made a generous contribution to the character and success of many of us. This modest establishment, hidden behind an overcrowded ghetto, produced a disproportionately high number of success stories which would have been the envy of many a university.

(During the years my brothers and I attended, the relatively small roll included: Imanuel Jakobowits, who became the Chief Rabbi of the Commonwealth; Kopul Rosen, Founder and Principal of Carmel College – the first Jewish Public School; Ian Gainsford, Professor of Dentistry at King's; Lionel, Henry and Basil Stoll and Max and Charles Levene all became doctors and served in the RAMC; four chaplains, including my brother Sonnie who served with Wingate in Burma; my brother Maurice who served as a major in the RAMC in the Far East; brother Leonard, a chartered accountant.)

On the days when we ate our lunch at the Yeshiva, we would sit round in a group discussing with the principal, who was nicknamed Kelly, the difficulties of finding a job with Saturdays off, and the chances of Hitler being murdered. One of the senior students, a good-looking twenty-year-old, would invariably sit alone with his back to the rest of us. For some time Maurice and I firmly believed that he was obsessed with meditation. Then one day we discovered that he was using a small mirror and the reflection of the sun to attract laundry girls who were having their lunch on a nearby roof. This theological rake eventually took an Honours degree in Homoletics and became a highly qualified roué A few years after we first met him he lost his life serving with Wingate's army in Burma.

The Sunday after we bade farewell to the recruiting enthusiast from Mir, we were given a rare treat. Our eldest brother, Sonnie, who was a senior student at Thrawl Street, was instructed by Father to take us out to lunch. This was readily recognized as compensation for an uncomfortable experience, but the recollection of the enormous pleasure derived from the occasion puts our life-style in perspective.

Three or four minutes' walk from Yeshiva, in the vicinity of Wentworth Street market, was a restaurant under the ownership and management of a Mrs Cohen. This inconspicuous establishment must have seen better times long before we were born. The décor, the furniture and the cutlery could have been designed by Chekhov, but only a Danny Kaye could have created the atmosphere. Here in the back street of a prewar ghetto, where the soup was more solid than the ceiling and a table-cloth was a word in a dictionary, service was the hallmark of the establishment and music the laughter of the customers.

This was the restaurant to which Sonnie introduced us for a three-course lunch. It cost less than a shilling each, including a one penny tip. This remarkable feat was achieved by the amazing Mrs Cohen and her aide-de-camp-cum-entertainer-cum-waitress-cum-manager-cum-cleaner, Doris. 'She'd make a wonderful gym teacher,' Maurice said, when he first saw this happy, blond extrovert bowl a fast roll straight down the centre of the restaurant into the hands of a regular customer. The uninitiated would have their orders passed down the line of patrons with a discipline that only Doris could muster. The old man sitting at our table shook his head as he watched a roll in flight. 'My poor wife, God rest her soul, used to throw things,' he announced nostalgically. 'You know,' he continued, 'maybe that's why I still walk with my head down.'

The roar of laughter that greeted his remarks encouraged him to continue. 'Imagine what Doris, bless her, could have done on the Western Front with a hand-grenade. The war would have been finished in 1916.'

'Harry, your soup's getting cold,' shouted an old customer from down the line.

'It must be against the Religion to dig up such dead potatoes,' complained a man who was shaking his finger at his vegetables.

'Can you imagine what a javelin thrower she would have been?' the old man asked the table. The question was never answered because too many other conversations were attracting our attention.

'In my financial position,' philosophized an impoverished

diner who had managed to secure a second helping of pudding, 'in my financial position,' he repeated for the benefit of those who might not have heard him the first time, 'I can only get richer. I don't lose any sleep over affluence.'

'So what keeps you awake?' called a humorist from another table.

'Shout your order over, darling,' yelled Doris, obviously addressing Sonnie. He yelled back for three eggs, chips, and butter, the bread already being on the table.

'You'll have soup,' was the response. It was a statement, not a question. It was obviously an unwritten law of the house that when you came to Cohen's, you had Mrs Cohen's soup. It was always a generous portion of good, thick, vegetable soup, served in a large plate. Although it was transported by the normal route, via the hands of half the customers, it managed to arrive steaming hot.

'You should never have my troubles,' the old man at our table said confidentially to Maurice. The latter nodded his head and, like his brothers, waited for the rest of the monologue. 'I'm suffering from incurable atheism,' he confessed.

This left Maurice and me lost for comment, but Sonnie quietly accepted the challenge. 'Who have you consulted?' he asked.

The old man studied our faces for a few minutes, put his soup spoon down on the bare table, and said knowingly, 'I've had to accept the condition as an act of faith. Otherwise, I'd be a very bitter man.'

This profound statement was over our heads and its subtle significance escaped us for many years.

'It's a shame to let your soup get cold,' Maurice said. This made the old man smile and shake his head yet again.

'It was a shame to kill the cow,' announced the potato joker, waving his index finger at his meat.

'Coming over,' shrieked Doris, as she released another roll from base.

The Seventh Day

'You should have seen the chickens we ate in Minsk,' said the man behind me to nobody in particular. 'In Minsk,' he recalled loudly, 'you needed a strong man to kill a chicken. Here, they die of starvation.'

'Three plates of eggs and chips,' screamed Doris as they were handed down the line to our table. The portions were enormous, but the old man still shook his head at the plates.

'In this country, that's enough for young men?' he asked rhetorically. 'They must make a fortune in this place.'

It was not until some time later that we learned that one table at Cohen's was always reserved for those in genuine need of a meal. It was never the same table and Mrs Cohen was never known to query the request. These two ladies had a certain charisma which made their customers feel privileged to eat at their restaurant.

'It's like eating in a circus,' Maurice said, summarizing the thoughts of the three of us.

A large man who had remained silent throughout the lunch suddenly began reciting a long version of grace after meals.

'It's an insult to expect God to hear in this place,' said the old man.

'Maybe the man feels he has to,' Maurice offered, thinking the remarks had been addressed to him.

'Feels?' yelled the old man. 'Who can do what he feels like? This ain't the world to do what you feels like. That's only in the next world, my son.'

'What do you know about the next world?' asked the food-flicker.

The reply was drowned by the voice of the man who was now singing grace. The only sound that rose above the noise was a voice that constantly screamed. 'Coming over.'

There have been few outings to restaurants since that could compare with our first visit to Cohen's. There were no carpets, no serviettes, no table-cloths and practically no staff, but its rich atmosphere compensated for all the deficiencies. We were very grateful to Father and Sonnie that day. This exciting experience was a source of amusement for us for a long time and we were able to think of the Man from Mir in perspective.

'He's a bit like old Mr Leib, only younger,' Maurice suggested kindly.

'Mr Leib doesn't wear clothes like that,' I reminded him. But Maurice was not to be corrected easily.

'Maybe he doesn't. But maybe his father did and he could have looked like that.'

In fact, Maurice was quite right. It was not too difficult to imagine old Mr Leib Rubensky originating in a place like Mir. He had arrived from Lithuania on one of the last onion boats to reach London docks at the turn of the century. To everyone, he was known as Reb Leib, the silversmith, a man amongst men.

When we first met him, the deep lines which ran down his face to his long, white beard, gave him the appearance of an ageless patriarch. When he spoke, his gentle, melodious voice added charm to his strange, foreign accent. He was already very old and we were barely in our teens. He had only one child, born to him very late in life, whom he called Isaac. The old man had prayed that his only son would become a great rabbi, but to his distress, Isaac developed an allergy to ritualistic orthodoxy and became a successful salesman. He changed his first name to Jack and enjoyed considerable popularity as a jovial, straight-dealing character.

The old man never tired of telling us the story of his father who sold his coat to help a poor widow keep the bailiffs away.

'His only coat?' Maurice had asked in amazement.

'Of course, his only coat,' he'd laughed. 'Who needs more than one coat?'

'Wasn't he frozen?' I asked each time he told the story.

The old man would take his grey beard in his fist and smile. 'You know, mine boy,' he said, shaking his head, 'It wasn't easy being a Rubensky in Sollent. Not at all easy,' he con-

The Seventh Day

tinued. 'You see,' he explained slowly, 'if you were a Rubensky, you remembered to behave like a Rubensky and if you weren't a Rubensky, you tried to behave like a Rubensky.'

This story had sounded wonderful to us although we did not fully appreciate the significance of his message for some years. I had taken his arm and pressed him to keep talking.

'Mr Leib, how did a Rubensky behave?'

'We-e-ll,' he began slowly. 'Let me tell you about mine uncle Pinchas. Every day, except on the Sabbath, winter and summer, mine uncle Pinchas would walk four kilometres to a Morning Service. He said he felt it made the deed greater to make such an effort rather than go two doors from his own home for the same purpose.

' "Uncle Pinchas," I'd say, "Why don't you take the horse on such a cold morning?" and he stroked his beard and shook his head and continued slowly, "You know, mine boy," my uncle used to say, "the horse doesn't have to attend services". What he was telling me was that every man has to perform his own good deeds. A second-rate effort was not for a Rubensky. A Rubensky never gambled with good deeds.' He had then mumbled for the thousandth time, 'Oh, Isaac, what sort of Jew are you? With your family, what are you doing for your people?'

On weekdays, when Father sometimes took us to morning service, we would stand next to old Mr Leib. Although many of the congregants would bellow out their prayers, we would recite ours quietly; partly because we were taught that way, but mainly, I suspect, because we were afraid of advertising our reading mistakes.

'Don't worry,' said the old man, one day. 'The Almighty also has an ear for quiet prayers.'

Invariably, as we left the synagogue, Mr Leib would take a bag of bread from his pocket and we would all feed the pigeons together. 'God also made the birds,' he would say. 'Why he made them, I don't know, but perhaps it was just to make some men stop and ponder a little while . . . perhaps.'

Desperately conscious of the examples which had been passed down throughout the generations of his family, it worried him greatly that he might be held reponsible, by the Almighty, for not impressing the Message adequately on his son. In his business life he was meticulously correct and at the end of each working day, he would deduct a tenth of his meagre profit for charity. 'Who knows,' he would mutter, 'what plan the Almighty may have designed for me for tomorrow.' As usual, he would look up to Heaven and, clasping his hands, would sigh, 'Oh, Isaac.' Just before his death, old Mr Leib Rubensky told his son to pray only for God's sake or for his own sake. 'Never pray for your father's sake,' he said.

When he died, Maurice and I were very upset. 'We've lost a friend,' Maurice said.

Years later, in 1949, a memorial was erected in Jerusalem in memory of those who laid down their lives rescuing Jews from German concentration camps in Europe. The name at the top of the list is Colonel Isaac Rubensky.

The story of the Man from Mir almost paled into insignificance, but tales of Cohen's restaurant remained favourites for years.

'Doris yelled like an army sergeant-major,' Maurice would say whenever she was discussed. This in itself would amuse the older members of the family who knew that the cover of *Picture Post* was the nearest he had ever come to such a character. Father would have found the analogy more acceptable if Cohen's had boasted a flag-pole.

At school, my Gentile friends found the tales of this East End restaurant quite hilarious. In a strange way, they were intrigued that a member of the class had discovered such an amusing place in the City of London. The headmaster appreciated the stories until a boy who was reprimanded for speaking during prayers, declared, 'I'm an incurable atheist, sir.'

Unlike the old man whom he quoted, this boy was cured with two strokes of the cane.

IV
Applied Chemistry

The stresses and strains of school life are more than enough for the average young boy. I was no exception, particularly as my academic progress was travelling in neutral at that time. The long journeys to and from school, the syllabus itself and the pressure of my religious education, absorbed practically all my time and attention. It was, therefore, almost impossible for political or social events to penetrate my little world with any impact. There were one or two major exceptions, one of which I have always remembered distinctly because it nurtured a prejudice and fostered a hate which left my memory scarred for life.

Believing that my mother was alone in the lounge, I barged in to find her sitting on a sofa in tears, with my father marching up and down the room. He appeared completely unaware of the interruption.

'The matter will be brought before the League of Nations,' he said heatedly.

'I just don't believe it,' my mother said. 'People should stand and watch and the police do nothing. Absolutely nothing,' she wept.

I could not fathom what they were talking about. It all sounded like a matter that was really too big for our family, anyway. 'What's happened?' I asked innocently.

They both stared at me, speechless, until my father said, 'You tell him.'

My mother wiped her eyes and burst out, 'The Germans have ransacked all the synagogues. They've burnt our holy books. Some of the finest work written by Jews has been destroyed. This is a day of mourning,' she sobbed, and she meant it.

It was difficult to know what to say or do. All I knew was that I couldn't have a conversation with my mother if she cried, but I had to say something. 'What are the Germans like?' I asked the room. 'What are they like?' my father yelled as though I should have known. 'They're uncivilized fiends, that's what they're like,' he said.

'They were the most cultured nation in Europe,' my mother sobbed. 'They produced Goethe and Heine and Beethoven and so many of the great theologians.'

'Was Hitler there?' I asked suddenly.

'Hitler!' my father shouted. 'Unless the League of Nations steps in now, he could become the biggest two-faced butcher the world has ever known,' he prophesied.

'The books!' my mother repeated continually. 'A cultured nation should allow such a thing!'

'If the German people do nothing now, history will not judge them guiltless,' my father said. 'No people can perpetrate such crimes and escape retribution.

It was all too much for me and I quietly left the room in search of a confidant nearer my own age. My eldest brother, whom I considered an authority on most things, was not home and I felt the younger members of the family were really too young. In order to vent my feelings, I sat down in the morning-room and wrote an address to Hitler, in verse. The following morning, I rose early to rewrite it, and I took it to school. The headmaster read the poem aloud in assembly and awarded me a house-point.

As I walked out of the hall, one of the older boys asked aloud, 'What made you write a poem like that? You're not a German!'

I didn't know how to tell him. I only knew he wouldn't understand.

That afternoon, as I walked home from school, I felt I had to speak to someone about the infamous German demonstration of anti-Semitism. At the age of eight, I found it impossible to place the magnitude of the event in perspective. Freddy Chapman, our family shoe-repairer, had listened to my tales of woe ever since I was old enough to walk into his shop.

'What's wrong?' he greeted me as soon as I pushed open his door.

I told him the whole story and waited for his sympathetic reaction. 'What a damn silly thing to do,' he said, without emotion. 'They could have sold all those rare books abroad and made a fortune.'

It was not the response I needed and I knew there was nothing left to say to him that day. Poor Freddy was killed on the beaches of Dunkirk only a few years later.

As I approached our house, I saw Jack Ewing, a boy a few years older than myself. 'Jack,' I said, very seriously. 'That was a shocking business in Germany the other night, wasn't it?'

He nodded his head, but he looked rather confused. 'Any of your family lost anything?' he asked.

'No, not *my* family,' I answered.

'Anyone you know?'

'No, but. . . .'

He never let me finish. 'You can't worry about everybody,' he said philosophically. I said nothing. I didn't know how to tell him that I wasn't worrying about everybody, I was worrying about Jews in Germany and the League of Nations and my parents being so upset. I was also worried because I was unable to define a new experience which later became known as Jewish chemistry — the strange, human reaction which is aroused in a Jew when he learns that other Jews are in trouble. I didn't know how to tell Jack that because it was still a mystery to me. It was probably still a mystery to him when his RAF bomber was shot down over the Ruhr in 1944.

Jack was a good friend who was always asking questions about the Jewish religion. Understandably, he found it difficult to appreciate how my father was prepared to walk several miles on a Saturday to visit a sick congregant, but would ask Jack to stoke the fire for us. Attempting to explain how the Talmud defined work was even harder than making him understand our dietary laws.

'We don't eat unkosher meat because we don't eat unkosher meat,' Maurice once told him impatiently and, to our surprise, Jack found the explanation acceptable.

When he played football for his school, I went to cheer for him, and when I swam for mine, he cheered for me. Apart from Christmas, Jack knew far more about our religion than about his own and he was happy to spend most of his leisure time in our house.

'You know the real difference between us?' he once said thoughtfully. 'I live in a nicer home than yours but you live in a family.' It was about the most complimentary remark that any of our friends had ever made to us and I was proud to repeat it to my parents. Jack's parents owned a dance-hall, where his father was the band-leader. We had absolutely nothing in our backgrounds in common but we were great friends and our door was always open to him.

It is interesting to recall that he was obviously much better off financially than we were, but it seemed completely unimportant at the time. Somehow we knew that he had several pairs of shoes and two pairs of football boots, but I cannot remember its ever being discussed. In the light of one particular incident it is surprising that we did not find these facts more significant.

V
Thinking Poor

There was nothing like a good, solid pair of rubber wellington boots to help a young boy trudge home from school on a wet winter afternoon. It is indeed a fortunate possession when snow and ice abound and ordinary shoes make walking a perilous exercise. But this particular afternoon was in the middle of summer and I was wearing my black wellingtons simply because my only pair of shoes was being repaired. My socks were already sticking to my feet which made me walk more slowly than usual. Maurice was obliged to reduce his pace but made only an indirect reference to my discomfort.

'Are we very poor?' he asked suddenly.

I was absolutely shocked that such an idea should even enter his head and at the age of ten I could not imagine what had prompted his question. 'Poor?' I exclaimed. 'Good Lord, no. We're not poor.'

'Are you sure?' Maurice persisted. I looked at him walking with his hair curling round his school cap and his eyes directed thoughtfully, at the paving stones.

'Sure?' I asked rhetorically. ''Course I'm sure.'

Maurice said nothing, which told me that he remained unconvinced.

'Look,' I started, in the patronizing tone reserved for younger brothers, 'I heard on the radio that last week one hundred thousand Chinese children died of starvation. They were poor.' He still said nothing, but I noticed that he had taken his eyes off the paving stones and was looking at my wellingtons. I knew what he was thinking. He had that funny way of telling you something without opening his mouth. 'A boy with two pairs of shoes isn't rich, you know.' I answered his looks defensively, 'and I only have one pair less than that. You're not poor with one pair of shoes and a good pair of wellingtons,' I said reassuringly, half to myself.

'I'm not Chinese,' Maurice mumbled to himself. Then in his normal tone, sensing my obvious discomfort, he asked, 'Where are you going to take your socks off?' We both knew what he meant and I was embarrassed that he found it necessary to ask the question.

'Probably in the garden.'

'Good,' was all he said and I realized his relief, as we shared a room together.

We children took all our meals in the morning-room except for Friday evening and Saturday lunch, when we ate together with our father in the dining-room. It was only at such times that a table-cloth was used. The rest of the week the morning-room table was covered with a floral-design oilcloth which seemed to last throughout our childhood years. On this particular afternoon, Maurice and I tore through the door to the morning-room shouting, 'Mama, hullo!' and we stopped dead in our tracks.

Half the oil-cloth was covered with a spotlessly laundered white cloth. A place for one was laid with our best silver and it was obvious that a meat meal was being prepared. But the real shock was the sight of the man sitting at the table. He looked like a tramp, dressed in very old, faded clothes, and he had several days' beard on his face. He smiled and simply said, 'Hullo, children.'

'Hullo,' we answered on our way out of the room, into the scullery.

'Mama,' I whispered. 'Who is he? What's he doing here?

Why the white table-cloth?' as though that was the last straw.

'You know,' she said, 'I've got no idea who he is. He came to the door and said he was unemployed and hungry. He knows he's a tramp; I know he's a tramp and you know he's a tramp. Just for once, I wanted him to feel like a guest.'

We said nothing because there seemed nothing to say. Maurice tugged my sleeve and we walked into the hallway. 'Is he poor?' he asked.

'At the moment, I suppose he is.'

'Is he Chinese?' Maurice asked, but I knew he didn't expect an answer.

Shortly afterwards, the rest of the children arrived from school and the six of us sat down at the oil-cloth end of the table to have our tea.

'I was in the war, you know,' volunteered our guest. This remark did not seem to surprise any of us as most grown-ups had claimed to have been in battle in 1914—1918. Several of us stared at him, waiting for his next remark, but none came.

'Did you lose a leg?' asked Maurice suddenly.

'No. Not a leg, thank God. I was gassed on the Somme.'

'Why?'

The tramp looked at Maurice for a long moment and answered wistfully, 'That's a good question, my boy, a very good question. A lot of people would like to know the answer to that one.' His eyes sparkled when he spoke but there was no bitterness in his voice.

'Did you lose all your money?' Maurice inquired, and again the man stared very hard at him until his face broke into a smile.

'There wasn't any money, lad. Nobody had money,' he added.

'Have your tea, boys,' my mother said, attempting to divert a conversation which was already becoming slightly embarrassing. But, Maurice was not to be put off. He frowned, took a deep breath and asked, 'Are you poor?'

Thinking Poor

'Poor!' said the tramp. 'Poor!' he repeated. 'Goodness, no! Temporarily without funds, maybe, but poor, I'm not.'

Later that evening, we lay in our beds with the evening light still coming through our window. My wellington-warmed socks were resting on the open window as I had forgotten to take them off in the garden.

'I'm glad we sleep in a back room,' said Maurice. I didn't answer him because I did not wish to renew the discussion about my socks.

'Funny, having a tramp for dinner,' I said, although we both knew there was nothing actually amusing about it.

For many minutes Maurice said nothing and then thoughtfully remarked, 'I don't know why he got gassed for nothing and I don't think he did, did he?'

'England had to win the war,' I answered wisely. 'It was the Germans who gassed him when he was fighting for England.' Then, to add a little glamour to the occasion, I added. 'That man who came to dinner helped to win the war, you know.'

'Yes,' Maurice said quietly, and after a few seconds asked, 'Are there lots of tramps who helped to win the war?'

I was as lost for an answer then as I would be today. Of all my brothers, Maurice had the most profound way of expressing himself from a very early age.

Just before he fell asleep he said, 'You have to be very poor to think you're poor, don't you?'

It was really a statement and not a question and I fell asleep in the happy knowledge that my shoes would be repaired the following day.

True to his word, Freddy Chapman had my shoes ready for collection when we called at his shop. 'I've used the new type of steel tips on the heels,' he said professionally. 'They'll last longer.' He spoke in the tone of a man who had analysed the problem carefully before reaching his decision. I expressed my appreciation and watched him put the shoes into a bag which had his name written on both sides.

'It's tuppence less than the full rubber heels,' he said. This was good news, but I was curious about the brown bags which had *Fred Chapman, Shoe repairer*, printed on them.

'Do you get more business having your name on those bags?' I asked. He obviously found the question amusing because he laughed an unduly long time before replying.

'In this street?' he said. 'No, I only have them because a new bag supplier does the printing for nothing.'

With my newly repaired shoes back on my feet, life again became normal and my feet were no longer an embarrassment.

VI
Timothy

The bus fair to the swimming pool was a halfpenny return. It was thirty-five minutes' walk each way and Maurice and I generally walked to save the money. The street was lined with a variety of interesting small shops which more than compensated for the exercise. In real terms, a ha'penny represented two sherbets, ten aniseed balls or one cigarette.

One February afternoon we had completed half the journey when it began to rain. 'It's not worth taking the bus now, is it?' Maurice asked, ever conscious of our economic position.

'Not likely,' I said. 'Let's go to the pet shop and buy a silk-worm,' I suggested, to get out of the wet.

'A silk-worm's not a pet,' Maurice answered in disgust. 'What sort of boy plays with a silk-worm?'

'They're for watching, not playing,' I explained positively.

'Maybe,' he conceded 'but I'm not prepared to pay for that!'

We walked into the pet shop and a tinny bell rang as we went through the door. The owner looked up and sniffed without enthusiasm.

'Place smells of dogs,' I announced too loudly.

'What d'yer expec',' the man said. 'It's a pet shop, not a florist.'

I walked over to the goldfish tanks and started tapping on the glass until the owner told me to stop it.

'Your fish are a bit nervous, aren't they?' I said defensively. The man took a deep breath. I pretended to be examining the white mice in a cage while I was quietly waggling my finger in one of the fish bowls.

'What the 'ell do yer think you're doing?' the shopkeeper asked angrily.

I looked him straight in the face and asked, innocently, pointing at a black-spotted goldfish. 'How much is that one with the measles?'

'That one,' he said, unamused, 'costs twopence and comes from one of the cleanest rivers in South America. If it's caught anythin', it got it from a boy from your school.'

I nodded my head and smiled as if the idea was a distinct possibility. 'Wha' else yer wanner know?' the man asked with an edge in his voice.

'How much is that poor puppy?' I asked, pointing at a bouncing fox terrier.

'What's poor about it?' the man questioned me with some amazement.

'Back leg,' I answered very seriously. 'Anybody can see it's got a limp, hasn't it?'

'Look 'ere, son,' he said lowering his voice, 'if you want to stay in my shop, OK, but don't make nasty cracks abou' my pets, see?'

I made a sympathetic expression as if I was trying to understand his problem. Just behind me, Maurice was examining the slow antics of a large tortoise.

'This is a real pet,' he said as I came alongside.

'A what?' I exclaimed, 'you can't call a thing like that a pet.'

Maurice looked up, put his chin out and half closed his eyes. He certainly looked a great deal older than eight at that moment. 'It's a special type of pet,' he replied emphatically. 'It's intelligent, it's different, it doesn't bite and it doesn't take up much room,' he added thoughtfully.

'It's the pet I want!' and he closed his teeth to make his point.

'Look at its neck,' I told him. 'It looks as if it comes from a leper family.' Maurice glanced up at me with a very superior look.

'The trouble with you,' he said with his head on one side, 'is that you don't know nothing about tortoises or lepers.'

The man was very amused by Maurice's attitude and was obviously impressed with his argument. 'That tortoise is one of the rare ones,' he said. 'Members of 'is family 'ave been known to live a 'undred yers.'

'That's all right if you want to live with a tortoise for a hundred years,' I said annoyingly.

Both Maurice and the man ignored my remark. 'How much is it?' Maurice asked.

'You can 'ave it for eightpence,' was the reply. We were both silent. Neither of us had ever spent eightpence at one time and, furthermore, we didn't have eightpence between us.

'I like it,' Maurice said, emphasizing each word. The man took a piece of white chalk and made a large mark on the back of the tortoise.

'You can come and see it again,' the man said kindly. 'You may even 'ave the money, one day,' he added knowingly.

We walked out of the shop to find the rain had stopped. It was too late to go swimming so we strolled slowly back home, looking at the shops, more out of habit than interest. '*Eightpence*!' I exclaimed suddenly. Maurice looked at me sideways and nodded his head.

'Yes,' he said, 'I'm going to buy it one day.'

The following afternoon, Maurice was late home from school. 'I've been to see the tortoise,' he confided to me.

'Why?' I asked, surprised.

'I wanted to see it again, to call it a name,' he answered simply and with a funny little smile on his face, he said: 'And I've called it Timothy.'

I could never remember having heard the name before and when I asked him why he chose it, he said, 'I thought it looked like a Timothy.'

During the next two weeks we visited our local grocer, Mr Finn, our shoe repairer, Mr Chapman, and several other tradesmen, in the hope of finding work to try and raise eightpence. It was quite hopeless. They all employed people prepared to work as long as they were needed. Maurice was too proud to ask either of our parents for a sum like eightpence and he persisted in his efforts to find the money.

'Would you like to sell your dog?' he bravely asked a neighbour who owned a pedigree dachshund.

'Sell it?' the man replied indignantly and looked at my young brother as if he were mad.

We went to the local railway station tobacco kiosk and asked people for the cigarette cards when they bought new packets. At that time, one could sell fifty cards for a penny. Unfortunately, our spare time did not coincide with the peak sale periods and we soon discovered the idea would not work.

'We haven't got anything to sell, either,' Maurice said as he took himself for a quiet walk.

About an hour later, he was back, looking very pale. 'What's a deposit?' he asked, very seriously.

'Why?' I wanted to know.

'The man in the pet shop wants a deposit of twopence,' he said, swallowing very hard. 'Otherwise –' he hesitated to grit his teeth, '– he said he may have to sell Timothy.'

Luckily we could cope with the situation jointly. We walked straight back to the shop and each of us gave the man a penny.

'You'll have to find the rest of the money soon.'

Maurice picked up the tortoise with the white mark on it, encouraged it to move its head and then put it down again.

'How much do you pay children who help you?' he inquired.

'Pay?' answered the man. 'They don't get paid, my boy, they do it for pleasure.'

'You can get impetigo from this work, can't you?' I asked rhetorically, in an innocent voice.

Timothy

'Look 'ere, son,' the man said to me, 'when you want pets, you come 'ere and when I wants a clown, I'll come round your 'ouse, O.K.?'

Conscious of his part-ownership, my brother visited the tortoise most days, after school. He gave me my penny back as soon as he received his next pocket money, in order not to complicate the question of title. The days drifted by and all the family became aware that Maurice was involved in a major financial transaction. It was finalized very shortly afterwards when my parents gave him the balance of the purchase price for his birthday.

When he brought Timothy home, we all agreed with Maurice that it *was* a very special pet.

During his first few months with us, Timothy paced out the length of our garden very carefully. Although a compulsive lettuce-eater, it was soon quite obvious that he preferred a good walk before breakfast each day. He was not a wanderer by nature, but preferred to park himself in one spot for hours, and silently meditate. Attempts by Maurice to train Timothy provided a consuming interest for months, but progress, if any, was remarkably slow. At one time, the family believed that Maurice had perfected a method of making his tortoise stick its head out of its shell without being bribed by a piece of lettuce. However, none of us, apart from its young owner, believed that Timothy looked any different when he smiled.

Sadly, none of us could have guessed that Peter, our fox terrier, would become consumed with jealousy over this new member of the family. At first, he would knock Timothy on to his back and quietly walk away leaving the poor creature flapping his legs in the breeze. As we were unable to cure Peter of this regrettable habit, Timothy was obliged to live in a cardboard box which was covered with wire mesh. Although somewhat limiting, Timothy appeared to come to terms with his enforced life-style and kept his spirits and appetite in good shape.

It was during his second year with us that he managed to escape from his prison. He was discovered, by Judith, re-measuring the length of the lawn. She expressed the view that Timothy had obviously benefited by the rest as she believed he was now walking faster. Peter seemed quite indifferent to Timothy and his newfound freedom and we were all happy to think that they could, at last, live peacefully together. But the goodwill was short-lived and on 11 July that year, Timothy was found beheaded. It was little comfort to Maurice that George Gershwin died on the same day. An appropriate funeral service was conducted and Timothy was ceremonially buried in a small plot, previously reserved for lettuces. Maurice swore that there would never be a Timothy the Second and he remained loyal to his oath.

VII

The Tea-Party

No doubt some years are punctuated by more significant events than others and their imprint on our memories reflects our priorities at a given time. The year Stanley Baldwin succeeded Ramsay MacDonald as Prime Minister witnessed a change in the political complexion of England, but it was hardly a world-shattering event. Pipe-smoking and national prejudices increased, but the world at large was more shaken by the invasion of Abyssinia by the Italian Dictator, Mussolini. The dismay and distress suffered by civilized people was further aggravated by the abysmal failure of the League of Nations to prevent or arrest the attack.

It was not surprising that these incidents did not really register on Maurice, who was eight years old at the time. However, that year did mark a flashpoint in his life, resulting from events which neither he, or I, had anticipated. For the first time, love hit Maurice in the form of Jenny Wilks, a pretty little minx who had fair hair, a trim fringe and all the wiles of a much older and more experienced flirt. She too was aged eight, but had a sixteen-year-old sister, Beryl, who kept her informed on the ways and weaknesses of men of her own age.

Maurice was a conscientious and gallant suitor and wooed Jenny with all the attention and imagination that his passions could muster. They would meet before and after school and Maurice would religiously spend the whole of his meagre pocket-money on buying her her favourite sweets. The pleasure he derived from this extravagance was enhanced by an assurance from Jenny that he was the only boy from whom she accepted such offerings on a regular basis. It was some while before I realized the extent to which Maurice was committing his time, his heart and his pocket-money, but there was little I could do without divulging his confidence.

'You don't understand,' he assured me each time I suggested he should reserve part of his pocket-money for other forms of investment or self-indulgence. 'I don't like sweets any more,' he lied unconvincingly, and continued to pursue Jenny Wilks to the exclusion of all his hobbies. This was no mean exercise, as she lived four miles from us and Maurice had to walk both ways, simply for the pleasure of staring at the outside of her house.

The great day arrived when Jenny invited Maurice home to tea on a Sunday afternoon. This was not a matter he felt able to discuss with the whole family, but he asked me to join him, largely to provide a suitable alibi. When the day came, we both gave our knees an extra scrub and plastered our hair down with water.

'Are you boys off to the cemetery again?' my mother asked, knowing our hobby of joining small funeral processions in the belief that it brought additional comfort to the mourners. We both laughed and left the house without giving a direct answer.

It was a dry day and we walked for nearly an hour before Maurice changed his cheerful expression to one of deep concern. 'I've got no money for sweets,' he blurted out. No explanation was necessary. Unfortunately, I could not offer any assistance, as the following day was pocket-money day and I was also temporarily out of funds. In any event, the idea of buying Jenny sweets had not occurred to me.

At that moment, we noticed a large cherry tree standing in the garden of an empty house. We climbed the wall at the

The Tea Party

rear and, standing on the top, we were able to lean heavily against a large branch and fill our school caps with enormous, ripe cherries. However, when we descended to the road, our hands and knees were absolutely filthy. The idea of arriving at Jenny's house in such a condition was completely out of the question. Furthermore, it was far too late to return home for a wash. After careful consideration, during which time we finished half a capful of cherries, we decided to make a détour through a local park and wash in a small stream.

To save time we began to run, but we had barely entered the park when we were hit by an unexpected shower. It was over very quickly, but in that short time, our hair had become completely drenched.

'Jenny will like these cherries,' Maurice said, oblivious of the effect the rain had had on our appearance. I stared at him, without comment, but felt that no girl could possibly be worth the discomfort we were suffering.

When we reached the stream, we each had a sock that had dropped to the ankle and the rain had taken some of the dirt from our knees down our legs. Unfortunately, the stream was practically dry and we were obliged to soak our handkerchiefs in an endeavour to clean ourselves. Our efforts achieved very little for our appearance. Having soaked our hands and knees with both handkerchiefs, we discovered that we had nothing left with which to dry ourselves. The effect was far worse than before we started. In addition, our hands were too messy to brush the tree-dust from our clothes. As a desperate measure, we turned up our socks to cover our knees and decided to keep our hands in our pockets as soon as they were dry. Regretfully, we had to leave our dirty wet handkerchiefs behind, as we had nowhere to put them.

We arrived at Jenny's house, nearly an hour late, with only one capful of cherries. She looked very surprised to see us and her sister, Beryl, inquired if we had been playing football in a pond. Mr and Mrs Wilks were not at home and it was soon quite evident that we had not been expected to come for tea at all. Beryl looked us up and down a few times and decided we should not enter the drawing-room as we might dirty the furniture. Not very graciously, we were directed into the kitchen, where we sat on the floor and watched Jenny eat all the cherries and spit the stones into Maurice's school cap.

'Don't you wash on Sundays in your family?' she asked in a superior tone.

We did not answer, but stared fixedly at a box of liquorice which was on the table. She read our thoughts without any difficulty, and, pursing her lips, she chirped, 'I'm not allowed to offer them to anybody, not even my *best* friends.'

It was quite obvious, from the look he gave her, that Maurice was sadly disillusioned with his little dream girl. Being disappointed was one thing, but his expression told me that he was definitely not prepared to be humiliated. Without a word, or a signal, we withdrew into a corner to discuss the next step. Neither of us was prepared to leave the house after such a performance without taking some meaningful action.

'Have you ever played hairdressers?' we asked Jenny a few moments later. The game which we had just invented appealed to her immensely, particularly as she was to be the customer. We sent her off to find a large towel and a pair of scissors. While she was away, Maurice emptied the cherry pips from his cap into a bowl which was half filled with granulated sugar. A few minutes later Jenny returned with a new table-cloth and a pair of nail scissors. Neither of us commented on her choice of linen which we considered immaterial to the exercise. She sat on the kitchen stool and smiled happily as we dressed her in the table-cloth and enthusiastically cut off several lumps of hair from the right side of her head. The effect was devastating, as it added a strong moronic dimension to her pretty face.

After making several unsuccessful attempts to even out the handiwork, we decided it might be wiser to leave. Jenny did

The Tea Party

not move, but sat there, dumbly, waiting for us to say something. Beryl came in unexpectedly and developed an instant look of horror on her face. She put her hand to her mouth and the gurgling noises she made convinced Maurice and me that this was not the time for conversation. We took our caps and walked out of the house as she collapsed in a fit of hysterical laughter.

We were completely relaxed as we walked home, feeling happier than we had done for some weeks. Maurice had seen the light and regained his freedom. I was delighted that we had survived the ordeal unscathed and had renewed our old relationship. Our pleasure was short-lived. As we entered our road an hour later, we recognized Mr Wilks's car standing outside our house. Neither of us had even considered this possibility and we dawdled round the block pondering on our bad luck and the alternatives which were open to us. Reluctantly, we agreed that there was no future in running away. Neither could we produce a defence that sounded adequate. Feeling more philosophical than brave, we walked into our house, after deciding that Mr Wilks was unlikely to leave without seeing us.

At first, my mother looked quite shocked by our appearance, but when she ushered us into Father's library, it was obvious that she was trying hard not to laugh. Both Mr Wilks and my father were smoking and neither of them looked the least bit amused. Father was standing with his back to the window and Mr Wilks was seated at the table, tapping his fingers irritably. We both knew that punishment was on its way and simply hoped that justice would be tempered with mercy.

'What have you got to say for yourselves?' Father snapped. Having agreed that our best defence was silence, we stared down at our shoes and said nothing.

'What a foolish, cruel thing to do,' he added in a slightly lower tone.

Mr Wilks stood up, put his cigarette out in the ashtray and glowered at us. 'You little fools,' he bawled. 'You could have done the child a terrible injury. You could have maimed her for life.'

Maurice frowned, put his lower lip forward and mumbled with a little pride in his voice, 'He was actually very careful,' and pointed his thumb at me. This unexpected remark took both men by complete surprise. When they laughed suddenly, we both knew that the worst was over.

We were sent to our room to write letters of apology to Jenny and her parents and we had no pocket-money for a week. Jenny appeared at school wearing a knitted green hat which came over her ears and Maurice continued to share his sweets with her until her hair grew again.

This short-lived romance might well have occupied our discussions for a much longer period had it not been for a major national event. The excitement which this caused both at home and at school put Jenny and her haircut into perspective. Nearly twenty years later Maurice met Jenny wheeling a pram round a suburban shopping precinct.

'Did your brother ever become a hairdresser?' she asked very seriously. The expression on her face and the question both called for a facetious answer.

'No,' Maurice said, as though imparting sad news, 'he discovered he couldn't stand the sight of blood.'

VIII
Jubilee Day

When King George V and Queen Mary celebrated their Jubilee in 1935 all schoolchildren in Britain were given a day off and the Mayor of our Borough allocated money from the ratepayers' fund to enable each child to buy a bar of chocolate and a fresh bun. Generosity of this order created history and occupied nearly as many columns in the local paper as the Jubilee itself. In reality, we schoolchildren were not just celebrating a national event, we felt personally involved in every aspect of the occasion. It was our King and Queen who ruled over our Empire and we were convinced that in order of priority, they were pretty close to the Deity. The National Anthem was not some majestic song for all occasions, it was a hymn which we all sang with the same enthusiasm as we would any prayer that implored God's personal co-operation.

Our headmaster suggested that each class might spend the holiday with a different teacher, playing in the local park, or exploring a nearby wood, or joining a magnificent sing-song with other children in the neighbourhood. This original programme gained unanimous support and was the subject of speculation and conversation for weeks before the great day. The atmosphere generated by the newspapers, our school and our parents gave the Jubilee a significance which negated any concern we might have felt for social or academic problems.

Atlhough we had arranged to meet at ten in the morning on

the great day, practically all our class had assembled in the park by 8.30. We were still to learn the name of the master allocated to us for the day. This was the surprise that was kept right until 9.55 when we saw Mr Samuel Evans walking smartly into the park. Our hearts sank and mine sank farthest of all. It had never occurred to a single one of us that we would be allocated one of the least popular teachers in the school and there was nothing we could do about it. As far as I was concerned, Jubilee Day was over and I simply hoped that the King and Queen would have better luck than we had had.

Mr Evans was a short, thin man with a strong Welsh accent and reputation for being consistently miserable. He taught English grammar throughout the school and pupils who found the subject interesting and could accept his idiosyncrasies, made progress under his guidance. Regrettably, most of us did not fall into this category, but nurtured excessive prejudices which were largely unjustified.

In my own case, our relationship had been distinctly strained. Our lines of communication were mostly crossed as I invariably obtained poor marks in grammar, which Mr Evans firmly believed was my intention. In reality, whilst I enjoyed English literature, I failed to grasp grammar, and no amount of practice or pressure seemed to help. The crunch had really come at the previous examination. The main exercise was to rewrite three desperately uninteresting paragraphs in a different tense. I was singularly unimpressed with both the style and content of the essay and, after reading it twice, I proceeded to write what I considered to be a much more exciting version of the incidents described. It was certainly a great deal more tense, and I was so pleased with my effort that I failed to appreciate that I had virtually ignored the question. Happily convinced that my carefully chosen vocabulary and my treatment of the subject would achieve good results, I was quite shattered to learn that I had come bottom with a mark of ten per cent. Furthermore, I lost a house-point, and Mr Evans

Jubilee Day

wrote a letter to my parents implying that I had intentionally misunderstood the question as a form of exhibitionism. Fortunately, the letter was received with some amusement, as my whole family knew that grammar was one of my weakest subjects and the general feeling was that poor Evans had over-reacted. I felt both hurt and offended and I discussed the whole matter with Maurice with a view to expressing my resentment very positively.

'My story was better than his,' I declared arrogantly.

Maurice scratched the bottom of his nose and sniffed. 'Perhaps you made him jealous,' he said, introducing a comforting thought that had not occurred to me. He looked thoughtful for a while and then told me a tale he had read in a comic he had borrowed. Allegedly, there was an African tribe that had discovered a cure for numerous diseases, bad habits and curses. The procedure was simply to name an animal after the sufferer, attribute the sickness to the beast and then sacrifice it with due prayers to the particular god of the day.

'It's known as voodoo,' Maurice informed me knowledgeably. The idea had considerable appeal for both of us and we agreed to experiment with the cure in the hope of making Mr Evans a more understanding and compatible individual. One afternoon, after school, we took a mousetrap and a piece of cheese and walked down to an old food store, near a railway siding. After some debate, we selected what we considered to be the most strategic spot, near a hole in the wall, and left our snare there. That evening, after a considerable discussion, we agreed that our animal, when it was caught, would be known as Mr Samuel Evans and not under any abbreviated title or nom-de-plume.

The following day, carrying a large bucket of water, we returned to our hunting-ground, to find a good-sized mouse in the trap. We declared, solemnly, that it was possessed with a mean, unfriendly nature, a bitter tongue and an evil eye. After repeating our accusations seven times, according to the instructions given in the comic, we encouraged the newly christened Mr Samuel Evans to enter the hereafter with a splash. Without procrastinating any further, we took the corpse home in the bucket and made the appropriate preparations to deliver the remains to their last resting-place. Both Maurice and I borrowed a stiff white collar from our father's cupboard, put them on back to front, and proceeded down to the end of the garden.

The unrehearsed ceremony was a drawn-out affair, as we frequently repeated our newly composed prayers for the sinner to be forgiven. We both avoided using the actual name of the Almighty in case we offended the Sixth Commandment. However, we did make frequent reference to the Powers Beyond and the Great Forgiver and felt confident that our messages would reach the right place without prejudice. A broken handle from an old rake was used to mark the spot and after chalking RIP vertically on it, we returned to the house for our tea. As far as we were concerned, we had completed a difficult and noble task with reverence and the matter was no longer in our hands. A little later we took our fox terrier, Peter, to the park and, over a cigarette, we discussed the ritual we had performed that afternoon. At that stage, lack of funds and opportunity restricted our smoking to one or two cigarettes a week.

Very shortly afterwards, as we expected, Mr Evans became unwell and a new teacher was appointed. My relationship with him was better, but unexciting, as he too failed to understand my inability to grasp the fundamentals of English grammar. The class all signed a card to Mr Evans wishing him better, but none of us was in any hurry to see him again. If one of the boys did miss him, the secret was well kept. It was only two weeks before Jubilee Day that Mr Evans returned to school, looking thinner and more pale than before his illness. The headmaster decided that he would take the senior students for the rest of term and resume his duties with our class when he was stronger.

We were, therefore, all the more surprised that he was allocated to us on Jubilee Day. He greeted us cheerfully and suggested that we make for a field a few hundred yards away.

'We can play rounders, potter round the park or sit in a circle and talk about things we don't like.' He laughed when he spoke the last few words and, to our own surprise, we all laughed with him.

The game was a great success and was so enjoyable that more than two hours passed by without being noticed, until Mr Evans offered to buy us all an ice-cream. At the refreshment hut, we saw four children about our own age who had their eyes glued to the ice-cream box. They were immediately included in our treat and Mr Evans invited them to join us for the rest of the day. We shared our lunch with them and when, later, we played 'Simon Says', two of them gained the first and second places.

Mr Evans told us that his father had expected him to be a miner in Wales and it was only his mother who had encouraged him to go to college and become a teacher. This led us all to discuss our own ambitions and dreams, and whilst most boys declared their aspirations were in the field of sport, some were positively enthusiastic about the Services. One of the strangers we had recruited thought he would like to be a comedian because he loved to hear people laugh and his friends said the idea of being a priest appealed to him, because nobody would interrupt him.

'What about you?' asked Mr Evans, pointing a finger at me. I hesitated for a moment, and he added, with a smile, 'Perhaps you could write exciting detective stories,' and although one or two boys laughed, I knew that from that moment my relationship with my English teacher had taken a new turn.

Mr Evans told us a number of funny stories about his boyhood and once he ruffled my hair and said, with a twinkle in his eye, 'We're not worried about tenses today, are we?'

I smiled up at him and regretted not finding a ready answer. 'You could use that imagination of yours one day,' he added quietly.

We finished the afternoon playing leap-frog and jumping backwards and forwards over a long narrow stream. Every boy felt tired and happy and knew that Mr Evans had been largely responsible for the success of the day. The cheer we gave him before we left for our homes produced a smile which we had never seen in the classroom.

As soon as I saw Maurice again, I related all the events in great detail. 'He was terrific,' I repeated many times, referring to our hero of the day. My eight-year-old brother stared at me through his half-closed eyes and a very serious expression came over his face.

'Voodoo works, doesn't it?' he said between his teeth.

Some ten years later, I saw Samuel Evans on Paddington Station dressed in the uniform of a corporal in the Royal Army Education Corps. His thin pinched face emphasized his pointed nose and I thought of the grass growing over a little mound of earth at the bottom of our old garden.

Jubilee Day was not only a historic occasion in our lives, but for some unknown reason it coincided with the time that we started taking more regular walks with Father. We would talk about everything in general and nothing in particular, but he never used these occasions to discuss religious dogma or discipline. Instead he would tell us stories of his relations of previous generations and their struggle to maintain a sense of humour in impossible situations. He related a story about an old uncle who had been forced into the Russian army in 1865 for two years' service.

At the end of that period, when he applied for his pay and discharge, he was given the money but told there had been a mistake in his contract. He was due to serve twenty years, not two. Uncle George signed the papers as he realized that the alternative was a long holiday in Siberia. He walked out of the Army office and, instead of rejoining his unit, he used his pay to buy a horse, and rode out of Russia into Poland. There he decided to sell the horse before continuing his journey to Germany. The dealer who tried out the horse complained that it walked too slowly.

'It was trained in a circus,' said Uncle George, to the delight of the horse-trader, and he clinched the deal. He stayed in Germany long enough to find a route to France from where he worked his way to England. He understood only a little English when he arrived at London docks, and when he completed the immigrants' form his answer to 'Race?' was 'No'!

Frequently, on the walks, Father came into his element when he spoke of Dickens. His enthusiasm for this Victorian writer was almost incongruous and was not inherited by any of his children. We were often surprised that a man who was not naturally patient could revel in the works of an author who wrote all his books in first gear.

Father became an authority on English literature and was as fascinated by Dickens as Mother was with Goethe. Although they did not really share the same literary interests, their attitudes to people and to those in need were identical.

IX
The Code

It was a long time before any of our family realized that the chalk mark on the wall outside our house was a code. Shaped rather like an arrow, it carried the initials GF, which meant nothing to anyone. The strange thing about it was that as the mark began to fade, someone would always draw over it again to renew its prominence. It was actually our milkman who enlightened my father.

'I should think that sign costs you a fortune, sir,' he said, sympathetically. Then, realizing that none of us had any idea what he was talking about, he added, 'That's one of the signs shared by the knights of the road.'

'Knights of the road?' I queried.

'Yes, young man,' the milkman answered, and raised his head and his hand as though about to enlighten the ignorant. 'That sign,' he said, addressing my father, one of my brothers and myself, 'has been put there by a worthy tramp, to let his colleagues know that your house is "Good for Food". In the next road there's another one marked NB which is "Nasty Bitch".'

At that point, my father thanked our learned friend and we proceeded on our walk.

'Shall I rub it off?' one of us asked.

'Certainly not,' my father replied very positively. 'You should consider it an honour that our house is known for its hospitality. I would never want to know that a hungry man had passed it by.'

'But Dad . . . ' I began.

'There are no buts,' he said. 'That kind of hospitality is a form of culture.' And then, as though referring to a priceless heirloom, 'It has always been an intrinsic part of our family life,' he added.

Whether it was the chalk mark, or simply a verbal recommendation, we never knew, but one of our most colourful and regular visitors was a shell-shocked cap-maker named Layman. He rarely referred to his trade but frequently spoke of his imaginary qualifications.

'Speaking as a philosopher,' he would say loudly, as though addressing a large audience, 'I do not believe Schopenhauer had any influence on Shaw.'

I was about twelve at that time, and very impressed.

'Chekhov,' he would say, suddenly. 'There was a man who understood poverty and desperation, but I will never forgive him for writing about it for money.'

His visits frequently lasted two hours or more and my parents would leave us children to entertain him most of the time. He enjoyed it as much as we did as we believed he was an unusual intellectual, and he did too.

'I would like to have spoken to Voltaire,' he told me one day, shaking his head with regret.

'What a shame he couldn't,' I whispered to my young brother, not realizing that Voltaire had already been dead for more than one hundred and fifty years.

'I too have had a perpetual nightmare,' he said. We were very impressed although we had no idea what he was talking about. 'Oh, my sorrowful bread,' he would intone whenever he joined our table, and we children would sit there waiting for the end of the prayer, which never came.

'Did you hear what Layman said?' I once asked my mother.

'It is *Mr* Layman!' she answered abruptly. 'He is a man who wanted desperately to improve himself and it is very sad that he should have to depend on others.'

'But Mama . . . ' I began.

'No buts,' she interrupted,' the poor are also entitled to dignity. He is Mr Layman,' she repeated. Thereafter, no one in our family thought of him other than as Mr Layman.

It was not long after one of these visits that my father and I went out for one of our walks. It was during one of my school holidays and I was delighted that he had suggested the idea.

'Are we going anywhere special?' I asked.

'You could say that,' he said, 'I have to visit someone and I thought you could keep me company.' He had that casual way of making me feel both wanted and grown-up. 'And how was our friend, the professor?' he asked, with obvious reference to Mr Layman.

'Fine,' I said. 'He seemed sorry that he had never met Voltaire,' I told him, hoping for some explanation.

My father found this extremely funny. 'Voltaire!' he laughed. 'They would never have got on, you know,' he said, as though he knew both men well.

'Who was he, Dad?' I asked, hoping that I might be able to share the joke. He looked at me and smiled for a moment.

'Well,' he began, 'Voltaire was a French writer, a rather unhappy philosopher who wrote some clever things for people who wanted to be miserable.' He paused and added simply, 'He lived at a very difficult time, in the eighteenth century.'

That little piece of information made me feel very knowledgeable, and when my father started telling me about his schooldays I was preoccupied, wondering how a man could earn a living writing for miserable people.

We had walked over two miles when my father stopped at a small row of shops in a very poor neighbourhood. I followed him into a grocer-greengrocery where he proceeded to order bread, cheese, eggs, tins of food, apples, potatoes and enough goods to fill two heavy bags. The bill came to seven times the cost of repairing a pair of shoes, a fact which I found particularly significant at that moment. When we came out of the shop, my father told me to wait for him and he took both bags into a tiny house nearby.

Some minutes later, he was back and we began our walk home.

'Who are the people you bought all that food for?' I asked him.

'I don't actually know them,' he replied.

'What do you mean, you don't know them, Dad?' I said, astounded. 'That was an enormous amount of food.'

'They're a very poor family,' he explained. 'The father has no work and his wife is expecting their fifth child and there was absolutely no food in that house.'

'What about the people who told you about them?' I queried. 'Why aren't they helping?'

'That's a good question,' he said. 'I didn't want those children to have to wait until somebody decided who was going to help them.'

I looked down at my shoes and said nothing.

'We always have enough to eat,' my father said, reading my thoughts, 'and your shoes will be repaired next week,' he added kindly.

'Do those people know who you are?' I asked him, suddenly.

'No,' he said, 'that's not necessary.'

I felt very proud of him at that moment and for some strange reason, I was glad we shared it together.

When we arrived at our home, I looked at the sign chalked on our house by one of the knights of the road. I never knew anyone else who had it, and years later, I thought it would have made an ideal coat of arms for both my parents.

X
Rachel

Before the days of the smokeless zone, a London fog would literally bring traffic to a halt and keep wise people at home. Walking through such perilous weather was both unhealthy and dangerous and even a torch did little to help prevent accidents. Nor did the fog prevent Cousin Rachel from arriving on our doorstep one February night. She was one of the most determined members of my father's wider family with a rare ability to take all challenges in her stride. She was short and neat, but quite exceptionally plain. Acceptable suitors recognized her finer qualities, but would not believe that marriage could possibly improve her looks. So she remained single long enough to realize that, in the matrimonial stakes, her odds were lengthening. But providence confounded the pessimists and, after a very short acquaintance, a Mr Nat Benson proposed marriage to her. He could not boast quite the same background as Rachel, but it was well known that Mrs Jenny Cayman of the East End was his aunt. She was the respected proprietor of Cayman's Kosher Kitchen in Wentworth Street. The food was good, for the money, but the establishment was renowned for its 'free table' which Aunt Jenny kept for poor guests. The quality and the appearance of these particular patrons did not do the business much good, but Jenny felt the exercise would secure her references in the hereafter. 'Jenny's table' became a byword wherever hungry people spoke of hospitality and though she didn't feed her relations, they all tended to trade a little on her reputation. So, in this way, Nat Benson was a Somebody!

Rachel had arrived to give us the good news personally. 'He's not so handsome,' she said honestly, 'but his heart is in the right place.' It was obviously a big occasion for her, but she still looked very plain.

'You are really happy?' my father said rhetorically.

'Happy?' she answered, 'I'm too excited to know if I'm happy.' She waved the palm of her right hand down towards the table and added, 'When I'm settled, I'll tell you how happy I am.' That was our practical Cousin Rachel. When she mentioned that her Nat was planning to take her to Rhodesia to live, my father sent Maurice and me out of the room. This was obviously a serious matter for discussion and not for children. We felt very humiliated and entitled to claim a degree of retribution.

At that time, the Post Office charged one penny for a telephone call and we decided to choose two numbers indiscriminately and complain anonymously about being sent out of the room to whoever answered. It was quite a momentous occasion as, usually, we only made one call, so we shook hands to seal our secret. I dialled the first number and explained that we had parents who did not understand us. The man at the other end thought it was extremely funny and hung up. Maurice made the second call and started with the same approach to the lady who answered.

'Perhaps it is very private,' the lady suggested tactfully.

'It can't be so private,' Maurice answered. 'I'm a member of the family.' This logical response caused considerable amusement and encouraged Maurice to add, 'It's not the first time you see. We have had this trouble before.'

'Maybe your father's cousin can't speak in front of a lot of people,' was the helpful comment.

Maurice sighed with a resigned nodding of his head. 'Maybe,' he replied slowly, 'only another boy could understand how we feel about it.'

'Who are you?' came the question over the phone.

Maurice hesitated for a moment and then with a mischievous smile said, 'I'm the younger one,' and hung up.

Later we spent some time thinking of all the clever things that could have been said, but we agreed that another call would make Father's punishment too severe.

The following day, Cousin Rachel was still with us as the weather had been too bad for her to travel home the previous night. We gathered that after we left the room she had spent some time discussing Rhodesia and her own parents' vulnerable financial position. For the past few years she had made a very good income from buying well-bound books in east and north London and selling them to Bond Street dealers. The margin of profit was substantial and she could never understand why the dealers did not compete with her. The result was that she was able to supplement her father's income and save up for her own future. She accepted the advice my father gave her and set off to make arrangements for the wedding.

'Does she look like anybody we know?' Maurice had asked my mother, with tactful reference to her unfortunate appearance.

'Cousin Rachel looks like herself, like we all do,' was the answer, but mother obviously found the question amusing.

Soon afterwards, we were all shocked to hear that Mr Nat Benson had left the country for Rhodesia without a word to Cousin Rachel or anyone else in our family. A lot of very unkind things were said about him and references to Jenny Cayman's Kosher Kitchen would not have been well received at the Pearly Gates. But Cousin Rachel spoke to no one and simply continued shopping for her bottom drawer. Two months later, against everybody's advice, she took another ship to follow her Nat. The following week, a letter arrived from him begging her to come out and forgive him. Her father opened it and spent a fortune sending a cable which told his intended son-in-law the whole story. When Cousin Rachel arrived in Salisbury Nat was waiting for her. It was a long time after they were married that he told her how he came to be there.

Some years later, when she visited England on holiday, she came to see us. During the conversation, when my father asked her how she had settled down, she said, thoughtfully, 'You know, George, I'm not excited, but I am happy,' and she really looked it.

'It's funny,' Maurice said after we had left the room of our own volition, 'I used to think she was ugly.'

Mother kept this remark in the back of her mind to quote to a Mrs Lamb who visited us quite frequently. She was a kind, generous soul who shared Mother's good nature if not her intellect.

XI
Days of Challenge

The Lambs always thought of themselves as friends of my parents. I can never imagine that they had very much in common, but Mr Lamb discussed his intimate family problems with my father and Mrs Lamb loaned her manual vacuum-cleaner to my mother. It was that sort of friendship. As the Lambs lived about a mile away from us, it was necessary for my brother Maurice and me to collect the vacuum cleaner together. It was that sort of vacuum cleaner.

One Saturday evening we were walking back from the Lambs, loaded with their domestic monstrosity, when we stopped to listen to a soap-box orator. Standing several feet above the small crowd, this mindless product of the English gutter made a very macabre impression in his black uniform. He was a member of the British Union of Fascists.

'Does he work for Hitler?' asked Maurice.

'I don't know,' I said, but I knew that he represented some kind of menace to decent society which I was unable to define.

In the background of my thoughts I heard Maurice ask, 'Why don't you know?'

'Hitler will save Europe,' bellowed the Fascist. 'Hitler is building a strong and virile Germany,' he yelled.

'What's he building with?' asked a dishevelled drunk who had obviously come in on cue.

'Ah! A very intelligent question,' shouted the speaker. 'Hitler is building Germany with Jewish money, that's what he's building with.' Then, pointing his finger in the direction of Maurice, who was then eleven, he screamed, 'It's the Jews in this country that have all the money.'

In view of our particular mission, we both found this statement amusing. Shortly afterwards, we left the meeting feeling that some adult should have said something.

'You would have said something if you could have thought of something, wouldn't you?' Maurice asked rhetorically, reflecting my own thoughts.

'England isn't Germany,' I said positively, to reassure both of us.

We did not say anything when we arrived home as we were forbidden to loiter. All the family were in the lounge sitting round our only radio set. My father removed his glasses and let his book fall on his lap as the BBC announcer introduced the news. A great deal of time was devoted to the confiscation of Jewish property in Germany, by Hitler, and the opening of more labour camps on the Polish borders. Britain had just agreed to receive thousands of refugee children, and volunteers were busy trying to place them.

'If we had money,' someone said, 'we could do so much to help.'

'It's people that do things with God's help. Not just money,' my mother replied.

'I think we should be proud and grateful that Britain has made this gesture,' my father announced.

'What's God doing about it?' Maurice asked aloud.

Silence hit the room immediately and we waited for one of our parents to explode. Neither did. Quietly, my mother said very simply, 'The Almighty has not deserted us for three thousand years. He won't this time either.'

Maurice sensed the tension he had created and did not pursue the matter, but still felt he should say something.

'We saw a proper Fascist this evening,' he declared, as

though it was particularly relevant.

My father looked at him for a long moment but said nothing.

'They're called Blackshirts,' my eldest brother informed us. 'Too many people listen to them,' he said.

That evening, Maurice and I discussed the matter very seriously.

'Our family will be doing something about those children,' I said, without any idea what I was talking about.

'How?' Maurice asked in a cynical tone.

'We're that sort of family,' I said positively, and I did mean what I said.

Maurice frowned when he posed his next question. 'Did you notice', he started slowly, 'Dad barely spoke this evening when we were talking about those children?'

'I noticed,' I snapped. 'But didn't you see him thinking?'

Maurice kept his frown well fixed and his voice controlled when he spoke. 'Yes, I did notice him thinking,' he conceded, 'but he never said what he was thinking about.'

The following day was Sunday, which Sir Oswald Mosley celebrated by leading a march of his disciples through the East End of London, creating havoc in the residential area extensively occupied by Jews. This was symbolic of the cultural contribution made by British Fascists at that time.

On Monday morning I boarded the usual bus to school. 'I listened to a Fascist on Saturday night,' I told a classmate who sat next to me.

'My father thinks there's some sense in what they say,' he replied, to my amazement. I looked at the boy and wondered what could make his father say something like that.

'What's your father's profession?' I inquiried, looking for a clue.

'He's unemployed,' he said.

For some unaccountable reason that answer seemed to fit the position and I thought I could understand it.

'I think your father will have second thoughts one day,' was all I could think of saying.

When we entered the classroom, the form master, Mr Evans, was already present. Standing next to him was a tall, good-looking boy with a rather sallow complexion and black hair.

'I want to introduce you all to Jesus,' Mr Evans said as we sat down. We all found this statement hilarious and, unfortunately, reacted accordingly. Mr Evans was neither amused nor flustered, but continued without reference to our apparent bad manners.

'The Spanish Civil War is not a laughing matter,' he said. 'Jesus is a refugee from Spain and we can all be grateful to the Friends of Free Spain that a hostel has been established for Jesus and some of his friends. This hostel' he said between his teeth, 'is a symbol of freedom on the one hand and hospitality on the other. You are very welcome here, Jesus,' he finished.

I was the form messenger that week and it was my job to take the new boy to the school store to be measured for his uniform.

'Is this a Communist school?' he enquired in good English.

'Communist!' I exclaimed. 'Good Lord, no!'

Jesus was rather taken back. 'Your father is not a Fascist, is he?' he wanted to know. Of course I found this very funny.

'No,' I said, 'we couldn't be Fascist, we're Jewish.'

'Funny,' he answered. 'I have never heard of any Jews in Spain.'

My journey home was spent thinking of my new class-mate and the Spanish war and the people who opened the hostel. But there was no opportunity for me to tell my parents about it that evening. Standing on the doorstep, when I arrived home, was my father. 'You'll have to double up with Maurice,' he greeted me, before I could say anything.

'What's happened?' I asked in surprise.

'We've invited four refugee children to stay with us for a while,' my father said.

'Four!' I bellowed at him, wondering how on earth we could afford it. 'Who are they?'

'I don't really know,' my father said, without raising his voice. 'They're just refugee children from Germany.'

Later that evening, Maurice and I discussed the events of the day with some concern. 'Four extra kids in the house isn't funny,' I said.

'No,' Maurice replied, 'but I expect if Dad had met Jesus first, we would have had five.'

In comfortable circumstances, a fifty per cent increase in the numbers of a household would be a major undertaking to be entertained with considerable reservation. To make such a commitment, with six young children, in delicate financial circumstances, would border on the irresponsible in normal times, but I believe at that time it reflected the unselfish and staunch faith which my parents shared. It was quite obvious that Father must have made his decision first and worked out the arithmetic later. With four extra young mouths to feed I have no doubt that our family budget was augmented by Uncle Julius who was a brother of my mother's and, at that time, a bachelor.

The miracle was not so much that we managed, but that we were completely unaware of additional hardships which the new members of our family created. Maurice and I willingly relinquished our beds and slept on mattresses on the floor and the whole family adopted our new members as a matter of course. Despite all the additional responsibilities which this obviously entailed, Mother still found time to maintain her correspondence and continue her theological and literary studies.

The children ranged in ages between four and ten and were able to cope with the language problem as their mother had received part of her education in London. They were all very cute and being part of an orthodox Jewish family fitted into our home very happily. Shortly after they arrived, a very good friend of Father's, the Reverend Tom Brown, called to see if he could offer any assistance. He was a local Protestant Minister and frequently met Father to discuss topical affairs and sermons of mutual interest.

'When I was a boy,' he often said, 'I knew I would be a Minister or a farmer. It had to be something to do with sheep.' And then he would always laugh loudly. He was very moved by the stories of the additional members of our family and the fact that their parents were still to escape from Germany. During the time that they were with us, he would appear frequently with vegetables and fruit from his garden. He would always make a special point of speaking to each child individually. Perhaps, more significantly, Tom Brown was one of the few clergymen, at that time, to use his pulpit regularly to decry the rise of Hitlerism.

At school, Albert Watts, the teacher responsible for religious education, chose to mention, in Hall, that my parents had temporarily fostered four refugee children. He made the announcement as a wonderful example of 'Christian' charity, but he could never have anticipated the sequel. Several of the boys were curious to know more about the immigrants, and my friend, Roy Huntley, offered to assist me in introducing them to the local park. He was the best-spoken boy in our class and had hoped to follow in his father's footsteps to Harrow. Unfortunately the family fortune was lost and, when I met Roy, his father was unemployed. He was a well-built boy, a year older than myself and captain of the football club. We were both in the gymnastic team and I would dive off his shoulders, through a hoop, and hand-spring off a high box. Apart from carrying me, he had to bend his knees at precisely the right moment to prevent my injuring myself. He was remarkably strong and very fit and I much regretted his absence when I was confronted by a school bully, Reg Blake. Accompanied by some ten other boys, he blocked my path about a hundred yards from our school. He was quite a good-looking, tall boy who had an unpleasant red birthmark on one side of his face. All I knew about him was that he had a reputation for scrapping, liked to draw blood from vulnerable noses, and was good at geography.

'Your father must be one of those stinking rich Jews to take on another four kids,' he greeted me, with a silly smirk on his face. This was the first time anyone had ever made an anti-Semitic remark to me and I was too shattered to say anything. I looked at the other boys and their silence told me I was on my own. There seemed no point in telling this crowd about Nazism and refugees and the emotions which led my parents to accept greater responsibilites than they could afford. I knew this was not the end of the confrontation and I just stood there racking my brains for something appropriate to say. Before any helpful thought crossed my mind, Blake pushed my shoulder with the palm of his hand.

'I'm dead right, aren't I?' he said loudly.

I let my left foot step back, to hold my balance, in case he pushed me again, but I didn't reply.

Apart from pillow-fights and the occasional friendly wrestling match, I had never been involved in any sparring activity. The idea of being provoked into a fight had no appeal whatsoever, particularly as I was quite sure that I would finish up with at least a bleeding nose. I had visions of standing in front of my parents, with a black eye, trying to explain the blood all over my clothes. In the same second I wondered whether to give Blake a hard shove as I was sure I would be no match for him in a fight. I also knew that I was not going to run away and be branded chicken-hearted for the rest of my school life. As I had no boxing experience, I decided that if a fight broke out I would try and swing a punch rather than throw it. A second, much harder shove from Blake followed quickly.

'You can't talk because you Jews are all damned cowards,' he scorned.

The force with which he pushed me would have knocked me over had I not positioned my left foot carefully. There was no time for any more thinking and the instant that I heard his last word, I stepped forward with my right heel hard on his left foot and simultaneously swung my right fist in the direction of his face. Blake took the blow on the side of his mouth and, as his body moved backwards, my heel momentarily pinned his foot to the pavement. He fell clumsily and when he tried to get up, it was obvious he had twisted his ankle badly. A trickle of blood was making its way down the side of his mouth, but he said nothing. I looked round the crowd of the other boys and without saying a word, I walked past them to the bus stop.

One boy patted me on the shoulder.

'He's been asking for it for a long time,' he said.

The thought that a boy from my school had made a derogatory remark about Jews distressed me more than the fear of being beaten up. It was not until I had been on the bus for some time that I realized that two of my knuckles were bleeding.

I arrived at the evening Hebrew classes late and took the earliest opportunity to give a detailed report of the incident to Maurice. I had obviously earned his respect, but the story worried him.

'Are there many Jewish cowards?' he asked.

I had never thought of the question and had never heard the subject being discussed. I didn't know if pogroms had produced cowards as well as heroes, but I did know that fear could not be experienced second-hand.

'A lot of Jews died fighting in the First World War,' was all I could think of to say.

I decided that I was not going to tell my parents about the fight for the time being. We felt that they had enough to worry about and I was determined that I was going to face this battle alone. However, as happens with many of the best-laid plans, it was not left to me to break the news. When we arrived home Father took me into his study. He could see that, for some reason, I was very close to tears, and he slowly lit a cigarette to give me time to pull myself together.

'Mr Blake has been on the telephone,' he said, smiling. He was obviously pleased, but I still did not trust myself to say anything. 'He apologized for his son's behaviour and said he got what he deserved.' He hesitated for a moment and then added, 'I didn't know we had a boxer in the family.'

Slowly, I told Father the whole story. I told him about the announcement in Hall and Reg Blake scaring the daylights out of me and how I would not be called a Jewish coward. I also told him that it was pure chance that my heel had come down on Blake's foot, but I was not afraid of him any more. He put his hand on my shoulder.

'I'm glad you didn't run away,' he said and then half to himself, he added, 'When there's so much at stake, you have to fight.'

When I arrived at school the following morning, it was quite obvious that many of the boys had already heard the story. My personal standing had risen considerably and congratulations came from the most unexpected sources. Several of Blake's chums assured me that they were really on my side, but I was not looking for their friendship. I vividly recalled their silence the previous evening when they had witnessed the whole incident.

During the day, the headmaster, Dr Dukes, summoned me to his office. I had only spoken to him twice before and on each of those occasions it had been in connection with taking time off for Jewish holidays. He was only five feet four inches tall, but when he spoke, everybody listened to him.

'We short people get underestimated,' he opened, staring hard over my head. He told me that Blake would be away from school for several days and that he would be formally punished on his return. A formal punishment, for a senior boy, meant a caning in front of the whole school. It was only administered twice during the entire time I was a pupil – the only other occasion was when a boy struck a master.

When I left Dr Duke's office, he opened the door for me. 'That move with the right heel might be worth remembering,' he said.

Some weeks later, I met Reg Blake in a little café near the school. He was sitting with a weedy little boy who was holding a cigarette under the table. He greeted me with the air of a businessman about to propose a merger. 'You and I could make a great team,' he offered, standing up. I raised my eyes and stared at the miserable red birthmark which was glaring at me from the side of his face, and I felt sorry for him.

'I already have a team,' I said and walked past him.

This incident was the only time I experienced anti-Semitism during my entire school life.

The four refugee children, who stayed with us for many months, were accepted into local schools in Ilford where they were treated with considerable kindness and understanding. They established a wonderful relationship with all the family, but particularly with Mother and our sisters. They all prayed even more than we did and had absolutely no doubts that they would soon be joined by their parents.

Understandably, Father was not as optimistic as these innocent children. News was filtering through daily of Jews being humiliated throughout Germany and of thousands who were being rounded up for so-called labour camps. Protestant and Catholic priests who protested or attempted to help the unfortunate victims were themselves arrested. Hitler's ideas for the Final Solution for the Jews were already well known throughout the world, but most governments were far too concerned with their own economic and political problems to be unduly sympathetic towards German Jewry. The attitude was not always a reflection of indifference or anti-Semitism. More likely, it was the ready acceptance of the creed that peoples of all races are expendable. Historically, this unspoken belief has brought comfort to those who feel that the relief of human suffering can demand too high a price.

From the moment the children joined our family, Father and Uncle Julius were determined to find a way of bringing their parents to England. The telephone lines in Germany were frequently tapped, but it was considered safe to make short calls to telephone boxes in the smaller towns. Uncle Julius had a friend who knew a man who worked in a German bank in London. He was sympathetically inclined because he had a Jewish girl-friend. Through him we learned that the children's father was obliged to report to the police daily simply because he had once been friendly with a wealthy Jew who had escaped from Germany with his own possessions. The children's mother had moved to the home of a friend because she was afraid of being arrested or raped by members of the Gestapo. The German frontiers were open and she could probably have found a safe crossing at that time, but it would have been extremely dangerous for her to try to escape together with her husband. Convinced that, in some way, she still had a job to do in Germany, she refused to leave alone.

Father confided his problem to the Reverend Tom Brown who swore that he would be as helpful as he could. Father also spoke to the Home Office, who were unable to offer any assistance at all. This infuriated Father, who bombarded an Under-Secretary with telephone calls until he was granted an appointment. This took three weeks to arrange, but he emerged from the meeting with the promise of two entry visas, if the couple could escape from Germany.

In the meantime, Uncle Julius had obtained an introduction to a Jewish banker named Joseph. He had a reliable contact in Frankfurt who had arranged for the children's mother to go into temporary hiding with a Gentile family. It was not only considered safer, but a member of the household worked in the police station to which her husband reported. Through him we learned that the husband was now reporting twice daily as he was on the list of Jews due to be moved to a camp on the Polish border. Father obtained some money from a few of his congregants and with the help of Mr Joseph was able to get it delivered to the children's mother. Important information was coming through various channels, but the prospects of getting the man out of the clutches of the German police seemed utterly impossible.

The German bank clerk offered to travel to Germany to assess the exact position, but wanted five hundred pounds for doing so. We knew nobody who had five hundred pounds for such an investment, but Father located the Jewish girl and warned her about her boy-friend. Tom Brown kept in close touch with the family but understandably had not been successful in recruiting any worthwhile assistance. He had spoken to the Salvation Army who had expressed sympathy and taken details of the case. They also advised him that the political scene was worse than it appeared and they were obliged to keep a very low profile.

Mother kept abreast of what Father and Uncle Julius were endeavouring to do, but as most of the ten children in the house were under fourteen, she had her hands full. Every day she ordered six loaves of bread and eight pints of milk and, together with vegetable soups, eggs and chips, there was always enough to eat. In the evenings Mother would sit down and try to guess which of the tradesmen would give her a little more credit to help her cope with a budget of a shilling a day per person. It was always an impossible exercise if only for the fact that there was never a time when she could expect any increase in her housekeeping money.

Among the many people Father spoke to was an old college friend, a German teacher named Gertman. He volunteered to visit Germany and arrangements were made for him to meet the father of the children in a little synagogue in Frankfurt. Gertman insisted on paying his own expenses and travelled on the overnight boat to the Continent. Thirty-six hours later he arrived at the rendezvous at night to discover that the Nazis had set fire to the synagogue. There was no sign of a congregant. The street was deserted and Gertman stood there staring at the smouldering ashes of a once-famous temple. After a while he bent down and retrieved a small Hebrew Bible from the rubble. It was beautifully bound but badly singed. As he slowly opened its pages he became aware of the loud footsteps of marching soldiers. He moved quickly down a side-street and stepped into the doorway of an old building. It was damp and cold, but one of the large alcoves on either side of the entrance served as an exellent hiding-place. He slid down the brick-work and sat on the stone floor and listened as the boots came to a halt.

'There's nothing left for us,' a voice announced.

'It's surprising the Jews didn't come for the ashes,' another voice laughed. A third man swore and cursed the fact that they were obliged to stand guard over an old building which had been wilfully destroyed.

Gertman listened to the miserable conversation and thought of his Jewish grandfather who had died in Berlin. He was the last full Jew in the family, but the relationship suddenly seemed too close for comfort. Stories of atrocities committed in German police stations were well known and Gertman decided to remain in hiding. He later admitted that he was genuinely interested in helping this sad refugee family but had no desire to become a hero.

The noise of retreating footsteps woke him from a restless sleep. He had been sitting in the same position for nearly eight hours. He felt tired, cold and, almost unaccountably, afraid. Only humanitarian reasons could have prompted him to make the trip and the fact that his mission proved unsuccessful in no way minimized his magnanimous effort.

The day Gertman returned to England, Father had two surprising telephone calls. The first was from a man called Charlie Snow who insisted on visiting us that evening. He was a very thin, clean-shaven man of about forty who wore an old blue raincoat and a grey trilby hat. His face was drawn, but his eyes carried the kind expression which parents frequently reserve for young children.

'The Salvation Army told me about your new family,' he said

as he walked into our lounge. Mother took one look at the man and disappeared to prepare a meal for him.

'I'm sure that man hasn't eaten for at least a day,' she said, as she took some eggs from the larder.

'What does he want?' Maurice asked.

'I don't know if he wants anything,' she replied, 'but I am sure he's hungry.'

Charlie Snow certainly did not want anything from anybody. He had cycled eight miles to tell Father about his modest charitable organization

'It has been established to help Jewish refugees from Nazi Germany,' he began. Father lit a cigarette and waited for him to continue. 'Just tell the parents of your children to pack up all their belongings and send them to this address.' He handed Father a piece of paper on which was written, 'German Relief for Poor Children in England,' and a postal address in south London.

'How exactly does it work?' Father asked in some amazement.

'It's simple really,' was the answer. 'Tell them to write all the initials of the children on the parcel and the number nine one zero. The Germans always let the parcels through because they believe it is good publicity.' Father stared at this poorly clad man in sheer admiration.

'Why are you doing it?' he asked gently.

The man put his head on one side and smiled. 'Rabbi,' he said slowly, 'I don't want to be ashamed of being a Christian.'

Mother returned with a tray with a white cloth on it. In no time at all she had prepared a large omelette, a plate of chips, several slices of bread and butter and a pot of tea. Charlie Snow ate slowly. He told my parents that he had thought up the idea himself only two years earlier and relied on the Salvation Army and one or two other charities for his information. He arranged for those concerned to collect their belongings and refused any payment for his trouble.

'What does nine hundred and ten stand for?' Father asked him.

'It's the ninth of October today,' he answered simply. 'It's a double check because it's the only call I've made.'

When he left, both my parents had tears in their eyes. They knew they had been privileged to meet a very great man and that our four refugee children would have reason to be grateful to him.

The second phone call was from Uncle Julius. He was calm and positive. 'George,' he said to Father, 'I'm leaving for Germany tonight.' The statement shook my parents.

'It could be dangerous,' Father said, remembering that his brother-in-law was a naturalized British subject.

'There isn't time to think about it,' my uncle replied. 'I've just heard that the man is due to be moved to a camp in three days.'

Father wanted to go with him, but he knew he had responsibility for a wife and ten children and Uncle Julius was a bachelor. There was very little to say and the conversation was over before it had barely begun. That night my mother prayed for the safety of her favourite brother.

From the time my uncle crossed the German border until he left Germany three days later, he was asked to produce his passport on thirty-eight separate occasions. He had been given the name and address of an eminent German doctor whom he visited as soon as he arrived in Frankfurt. Later, when he reached his hotel, he found a Nazi officer waiting for him in his room.

'Your passport, Julius Jung,' the officer demanded. He examined it and handed it back. He then sat down on the only chair in the room. 'I'm a friend of Herr Linkmann,' he said, mentioning the name of a businessman my uncle had been told to contact. 'If all goes well, the man you want to rescue will be in Holland in two days. If he is suspected, he will be shot and you will be arrested.'

My uncle knew that the other man was one of the very few German Nazis who were doing everything possible to help Jews escape. He also knew that if this particular plan failed, the local police would hold him in custody, British passport or not.

'What about his wife?' my uncle asked.

The officer shrugged his shoulders, 'I believe she is leaving tomorrow.'

That night, the father of our four refugee children reported as usual to the police in Frankfurt. When he left the station he walked to the General Hospital and collapsed on the steps. The same eminent German doctor was coming through the hospital doors at that moment. The man was immediately admitted to the hospital and the doctor diagnosed a contagious disease. The patient was placed in a private isolation ward for twenty-four hours with instructions that he was not to receive either visitors or treatment.

At three o'clock the following morning, the man got out of bed and silently slipped into the bathroom next door. There he dressed in his own clothes with a white doctor's coat over them. Wearing a stethoscope round his neck and a pair of pince-nez on his nose, he walked down the steps of the hospital into a waiting car. He was first driven to Cologne, where he stayed at a small hotel under an assumed name with the title of Doctor. The following day by a ghastly chance a woman fainted in front of him in the hotel dining-room. The manager was standing nearby.

'*Herr Doktor*,' he said, bowing, 'can you please examine this poor lady?'

The man kept his nerve, leaned over the woman, and pretended to use his stethoscope. 'Call an ambulance immediately,' he said calmly, 'she could be seriously ill.' He made no effort to revive the lady, and after a few minutes left the hotel. The following night he arrived in Holland. The Dutch never questioned a German Jew who was crossing the frontier.

During this time, Uncle Julius was arranging for the children's clothing to be sent to the address in England which Father had given him, on the phone, before he left. He also paid a furniture dealer to send several crates of personal effects to a sham firm of auctioneers in London. An anonymous telephone caller told him that the 'two actors had been hired for a new play' and he knew that both parents had crossed the German border.

When he arrived at Frankfurt railway station, the platforms were full of police and several were standing round each ticket office. My uncle walked slowly through the crowds to the train which was due to leave in a few minutes. It was already crowded and he knew he would have to stand for several hours. As he opened the carriage door, he felt a heavy hand on his shoulder. Before he could turn round, he heard a voice demand sternly, 'Your passport!'

He was conscious of gall moving up from his stomach to his throat as he drew his passport from his inside pocket. Slowly, he turned to hand it to the German officer behind him, and found himself staring into the same face that he had first seen in his hotel bedroom. Without a flicker of recognition the officer examined the passport and handed it back to Uncle Julius.

'No man could have a greater friend,' he said, without smiling, and walked away. No German ever uttered a truer word in that era.

A week later we had a tea-party at our home including the whole reunited refugee family, Tom Brown, Uncle Julius and our doctor Edward Beatty. Unfortunately Charlie Snow was unable to join us and we children never saw him again. A great deal of the discussion at the tea-table was centred on the number of Jews who were leaving Germany and the human problems created by this exodus.

'Will God manage to get away?' asked Trude, who was the six-year-old member of the family who were now planning to leave us. The silence that greeted the question lasted longer than was comfortable for any of the adults present. After many moments, it was Maurice who addressed the child quietly.

'Only God knows the anwer to that,' he said.

Thoughtfully, Father took the opportunity to propose a special toast to his brother-in-law. This was greeted with loud cheers from everybody and all the kids rushed to Uncle Julius to express their appreciation in their own way. At that moment there was a ring at our front door. Standing on the step was the German teacher, Gertman. Father had invited him, and although at first he had declined, he had changed his mind in order to hand over the leather-bound Bible to the man he had hoped to rescue himself. We all knew that Mr Gertman was a big man even though he was under 5 feet 4 inches tall.

XII
One Man Alone

It is perhaps strange that none of us felt even remotely deprived because we had neither a bicycle nor a train-set between us. On the contrary, we felt extremely fortunate that we boasted our own football, two rusty golf-clubs and a Go-Kart which my eldest brother, Sonnie, made out of a pram and an orange box. Imagination was probably our greatest asset in the leisure field, and sailing in a make-believe boat, made from two bed-sheets and three kitchen chairs, gave us more pleasure than any craft my father could have owned.

But better than all our possessions was our Uncle Julius. Even today I find it impossible to describe the effect that he had on all of us throughout his life. He had the rare ability to make children feel happy just because he was around and his infectious smile swept away many of our tears. 'We must tell Uncle Julius,' was probably the most commonly heard statement in our house, whenever there was any good or bad news to impart.

'He doesn't just share our pleasure, he helps to create it,' one of my brothers said and nobody would have disagreed with him.

Despite his trim, short figure, his modest manner and his quiet life-style, Uncle Julius was no ordinary linesman when it came to the game of life. He was not an armchair politician or crowd follower; he was a man who led the consciences of other men by spontaneous and impressive performance. Unfettered by bureaucracy or political ambition, he considered the cries of human suffering as his personal challenge. Perhaps, therefore, it was not so surprising that he was the only man I ever knew who mounted a one-man crusade to rescue children from Nazi Germany.

Hampered by driving rain and biting winds, he would tour the poor suburbs of London begging people to accept a refugee child before Hitler did. 'Any couple who leaves this synagogue hall tonight,' he would say, slowly and precisely, 'without a commitment, is sentencing a child to an unknown fate . . . like death!' he would add softly.

I was privileged to travel with him many times and would sit on a hard chair at an old wooden table, making a record of those who committed themselves.

'You only have to question if your hearts are big enough,' he would remonstrate. 'I'm sure you can find room in your homes.'

Whenever his words drew tears from the women in the audience, he would tone down his voice and say, 'You don't have to cry. You are the lucky ones who can do something about it.' And, looking round the hall, he would point at everybody and nobody and add gently, 'Please, please dry your tears. There are too many weeping parents in Europe already.' He knew very well that his words would provoke more sobs and stir the hesitant to add their names to our list.

One wet, winter night, we left a small communal hall in a poor district of London and climbed into my uncle's little Austin car. 'We got eighteen tonight,' I said proudly.

He said nothing as the windscreen wipers flicked noisily back and forth.

'What's the total?' I asked, wanting him to say something.

'Three hundred and four,' he answered in a flat voice.

I was about to congratulate him when he said, 'It's nothing! There are thousands waiting and there's so little time.' To this day, I am thrilled that he included me in his mission, although we both knew the size of my contribution. But that was my Uncle Julius.

'Does anybody thank you?' I enquired innocently one evening.

'Thanks!' he exclaimed heatedly. 'I don't want thanks, I want more children out of that hell-hole.'

There was no answer to that so I started on another track, hoping I might be more constructive. 'Uncle,' I asked, 'why don't we go to the rich districts, where people have large houses and servants?'

He exhaled slowly and then, shaking his head, he said, 'I'm afraid, my boy, you will learn that the rich find it very hard to give. You see,' he added wistfully, 'no one understands distress and poverty like the poor.'

He would spend hours every day persuading the British government to grant more permits or bullying institutions to expedite formalities. Actively avoiding publicity, and without regard for his health or his modest bank balance, he worked night and day to rescue children from the clouds of horror which were rapidly enveloping Europe. This was my Uncle Julius, a little man with a big conscience and an even bigger heart.

I recall, once, accompanying him when he was a guest speaker at some insignificant historical society. He had worked hard writing, rewriting and memorizing a long speech. Unfortunately, when we arrived, we learned the secretary had forgotten to post the invitations. There were only three people present who had been notified that same day. My uncle approached an ill-clad man who was sitting in the back row.

'How long did it take you to get here?' he asked.

'About an hour,' the man replied. 'I walked.'

My uncle returned to the table and gave his speech, which took more than fifty minutes to deliver. Two weeks later, he returned and gave it again.

As the years went by, he continued his fight for the freedom of the individual, regardless of the country of origin. When he was eighty years old, it was estimated that more than eight thousand men, women and children owed their lives to his personal initiative, to his drive and to his conscience. Most of all, to his belief that every man has the God-given right to be free.

When my Uncle Julius died peacefully, in his bed, I lost a great friend and mentor and I honestly believe the world became poorer.

XIII
Beyond the Fringe

One of the few luxuries which my mother allowed herself was the literary paper, *John O'London's Weekly*. It provided a detailed reading list for the family and for herself and its competitions gave her the opportunity to test her wide literary knowledge. As a result of her encouragement, the local library became our second home, and proper use of the English language, a recognized talent. For each one of us, reading was a delightful hobby more than an academic exercise, although our choice of books was rather carefully monitored. Whilst the recommendations of *John O'London's* lay around the house, Maurice and I kept the sleazy magazines underneath our mattresses. These were usually borrowed from our young daily help who identified all romantic disasters with her own catastrophic love life.

'I'm one of the wrong people to be educated,' she would often say, and then add philosophically, 'It would only give me ideas too big for my station.'

Her choice of magazines catered for her intellectual and emotional demands and introduced us to some fascinating social and biological problems somewhat prematurely.

Despite the trials and irritations which a large family produce and the problems created by a very modest income, I never once heard my mother swear. She spoke three languages fluently, but never extended her vocabulary to the borders of profanity. In this area we children could not claim to have emulated her, but we did, at least, have two categories of swear words, those used at school and a less expressive collection which we kept in reserve for home use. Even the latter group, which were very mild indeed, were not acceptable to our mother. When my father was really annoyed, his face showed it and he raised his voice, but I always felt he had a good store of oaths for his own silent swearing sessions. The odd swear-word that escaped his lips would probably be included in the vocabulary of a refined child of six today. If ever my brothers or I expressed ourselves in what was described as undignified language, my mother would say, 'Go wash your mouth out with soap.'

With this background, it was perhaps not surprising that Mother was never particularly pleased to welcome Cousin Rose. She was really a second cousin of my father's and was by a long way the best-looking member of the family. However, Maurice and I were always pleased to see her because she swore eloquently. Not the fit-for-most-ears variety, but the real healthy swear words which would be acknowledged as such in any generation. Strangely enough, Father never appeared disturbed by Rose's expletives, but Mother felt she offended good taste and did her best to keep us children out of hearing distance.

'There's nothing wrong with Cousin Rose,' Mother would say condescendingly, 'but she learnt the wrong language at school and now she can't forget it.'

We thought the explanation ingenious but unacceptable, and Cousin Rose remained our secret pin-up. 'She doesn't swear like the milkman, she swears like a lady,' Maurice explained to our youngest brother, Leonard, when he was five years old.

'Do all ladies swear so nicely?' he asked.

My mother was quite concerned by the tone of our conversation and invariably when Cousin Rose came on one of her rare visits, we were packed off to say night prayers earlier than usual.

This unique member of our family had a husband blessed with the name of Solomon Robert, but she called him Bobs. He was a round man with a bald head and a laugh that reminded me of the Big Top at the fair. Cousin Bob bought toys in Japan which he then brought back to England and sold to Woolworth's. He prefaced all his remarks with, 'I was saying to Rose the other day . . . ' He was a rather jovial bore and I suppose we only saw him half a dozen times in our lives.

One day, we learned that this unlikely pair had been divorced. It was the first time I had heard the word used in respect of real people. Apparently, Father had tried very hard to dissuade them, but his efforts had proved futile. It was not a subject for discussion in front of the children and although there was no other party involved, I never heard my mother mention Cousin Rose again.

Many years later, someone related a story of a woman who lost her husband in a Miami nightclub. Allegedly, he had consumed an enormous meal, pushed back his chair from the table, wiped his mouth with his serviette and expired. The widow quietly transferred his wallet from his inside pocket to her handbag and collapsed on the floor in a fit of hysterics. It was Cousin Rose bidding farewell to her second husband.

Her first marriage had produced a son, named Daniel after one of the children of Jacob. She called him Bill. He was an uninspiring individual who lacked the personality of his mother and the tenacity of his father. We never knew his occupation, but gather that he habitually changed his religion. He deserted Judaism in favour of atheism before becoming a Seventh Day Adventist. A year later he claimed to be experimenting in Spiritual Love by living with a woman twice his age. After several other changes he became a founder-member of the Children of Genesis and worked hard converting unsuspecting morons to the new sect. When he died, prematurely, in a motor accident, he left a few hundred dollars and a request to be buried in a Jewish cemetery. Unfortunately, the note was found several weeks after his funeral and he remains buried in some unidentified grave in California.

When I last saw Cousin Rose, she was a very old lady and she still swore.

XIV
Lost Chord

Apart from the occasional infatuation, I do not believe I was seriously attached to any girl until I met Daphne. We were both thirteen and team members of the school swimming club. This gave us a certain standing and brought us together at least once a week. She was an attractive, auburn-haired girl who had frozen so many of the boys that they called her igloo. After watching her closely for several weeks and thinking of her most nights, I decided to risk becoming a member of the igloo club, as her rejects were called.

The next time we met, she was just leaving school. I strolled along, next to her, in the opposite direction to my way home.

'I may have to give up the swimming club,' I lied, to provoke a conversation.

For a few moments we walked in silence and then she asked, 'Why? Is it the chlorine?'

I frowned because I really wanted to laugh. 'No,' I answered sharply. 'It's French. I haven't told anyone yet,' I said truthfully, 'but my parents believe that too much swimming can be bad for my brain.'

'Do you believe that?' she asked in an incredulous tone which warned me to watch my lies carefully.

'You see,' I started slowly, 'in our family, certain tissues are affected by the chemicals they put in swimming pools.' I exhaled and wondered if she would challenge the statement, but she let it pass.

Lost Chord

'But why French?' she asked. I was pleased to see from her big, blue eyes that she was really concerned about me.

'I'm bottom in French,' I replied gloomily.

'Really bottom?'

'Yes. Really. I was thirty-third last term and only thirty-second the term before because one boy was sick.'

By this time we had actually walked past Daphne's bus stop and arrived at a bench, near a large oak tree.

'I could tell my father that my French is much better,' I said in a worried voice, as we sat down. 'Or I could just leave the swimming club, couldn't I?' I asked, happily sharing the imaginary responsibility.

That was really the punch-line that began our romance. I sat there thinking of my expressive lie and Daphne sat next to me, looking very worried indeed. I was delighted with the situation and hoped that my imagination would not desert me.

'Are you bottom in anything else?' she asked suddenly.

'Geography,' I answered honestly.

'Why don't you give that up instead of French?' she enquired.

'I can't,' I said. 'I promised my grandfather,' I added for no reason at all.

'Why your grandfather?' I heard her voice pursuing me and wondered how long I could keep the story going.

'He was a colonel,' I lied more easily. 'He died of war wounds and he spoke fluent French . . . ' My voice trailed off, leaving the sentence unfinished. Daphne looked at me sideways, banged me in the ribs with her elbows, and started laughing until tears poured down her face.

'You're a terrific liar, a really great liar,' she roared. By this time we were both laughing so loudly that passers-by looked at us with amusement.

After that, we walked to our favourite bench, every day, after school. We used to sit together, touching shoulders, and I was really pleased that her hands were clammy because mine were too. Our conversation quickly graduated from the scholastic to the ridiculous and our emotions ignited at an ever earlier flash-point.

'I've got to get the early bus,' I announced one day as we were leaving school.

'Why?' she asked and I was flattered to hear the note of alarm in her voice.

'I can't keep saying that I missed the bus or had to go back for my books,' I answered sheepishly.

'I get into terrible trouble too, when I'm late.' She added cunningly, 'My father hates me being late.'

We walked a little way without saying a word. 'There must be an answer,' I said hopelessly.

'I can't come home late without telling my parents something convincing,' Daphne said in response. We walked on feeling that all our day-dreams would be punctured because our parents would never understand our problem.

Suddenly, Daphne blurted out, 'I've got a wonderful idea, a terrific idea!'

I just looked at her and waited.

'We could join the school choir,' she said happily. 'It meets after school,' she added, to explain herself.

'What on earth for?' I asked.

She screwed up her nose and her eyes with a mischievous smile. 'We could then play truant from it, couldn't we?' she laughed.

When I arrived home, all the family, except my father, were having tea.

'Late again,' two of the family greeted me simultaneously.

'I smiled and decided to break the news quickly, so that I could enjoy my tea.

'I'm trying to join the school choir,' I said casually.

'They can't be that hard up,' one of my brothers retorted.

'What made you think of that?' my mother asked.

'I didn't have an answer ready so I coughed while I thought

of one. 'You can get extra house-points for being in a school concert,' I said suddenly. My mother eyed me suspiciously.

'Do you have to miss any other subjects?' was her next question.

'Good Lord, no!' I answered enthusiastically 'You can't get away with that at our school. If you're in the choir you have to practise about three times a week after school' I added the last words as I looked round the table to observe their effect. I felt sure that my eldest brother and sister didn't believe me, but they said nothing. They were always nice like that.

Daphne and I continued meeting regularly. I found that I could make her laugh as easily as she made me feel that I was growing up. It was a happy, romantic and exciting time and even my studies did not suffer noticeably because I was doing pretty badly already. Often, we spent a while rehearsing well-known folk-songs and ballads which we continually hummed around our respective homes.

'Do you really enjoy the choir?' my younger brother asked me one day.

'Not really,' I said. 'But I think I'll stick it for a while.' It wasn't so much the question as the look that accompanied it that worried me. I knew very well that he didn't believe me, but I simply wasn't prepared to enlighten him.

A few weeks later, the long arm of coincidence dealt a mortal blow to our clandestine affair. As Daphne and I sat on our favourite bench on a July afternoon, I noticed one car in the line of traffic that passed us. Sitting in the passenger's seat was my father.

When I arrived home, no one said anything and neither did I. I also decided not to hum, to avoid bringing unnecessary attention to myself. However, while I was doing my homework, alone in the study, my father came in to speak to me.

'How are things going?' he opened in his normal voice.

'Not too bad,' I answered unconvincingly. He lit a cigarette and sat down with a glimmer of a smile on his face.

'Is your French any better these days?' he inquiried.

'No, dad,' I answered truthfully. 'It's no better.'

My father inhaled deeply and blew smoke rings across the room. 'Do you think you should give up the choir practice?' he asked with a twinkle in his eyes. At that moment, I knew just how much I really liked him. We both laughed and we both knew that my choir days were over.

He never referred to it again and it was never mentioned by anyone in our family.

XV
The Munich Crisis

When the Prime Minister, Neville Chamberlain, returned to London from Munich, having given the freedom of Czechoslovakia to Hitler, there were two serious repercussions in our home. My parents were both shocked, particularly my mother because she had been born in that country, and my father because he felt the last vestige of faith in the League of Nations had been destroyed. Bitterly, they were convinced that worthwhile values were deteriorating at an uncontrollable speed, and that decent people throughout Europe were becoming increasingly helpless.

The other problem created by the political situation was more local, but of serious significance to those involved in it. The day which had been chosen by Maurice and me to apply for an increase in pocket-money coincided with the day Czechoslovakia was deserted by Chamberlain. It was extremely unfortunate as our financial position had long been too delicate to balance with any degree of dignity.

'We can't ask him now,' Maurice said, recognizing that the domestic climate was quite unsuitable for raising mundane matters.

'It's quite impossible on fourpence a week,' I muttered.

'Fourpence!' Maurice exclaimed. 'After a halfpenny for the charity box and a penny for savings, what's left?'

Even though tuppence ha'penny bought five cheap cigarettes

or a comic and two strings of liquorice, it was quite insufficient to make adequate reserves for presents and emergencies.

'I'm going round to see Johnny Stone,' I announced the day after Chamberlain made his statement.

'We can't work for him,' Maurice said positively and I knew exactly what he meant.

Johnny was no great friend of mine, but he was by far the most entrepreneurial boy in our school and the only one likely to suggest a possible answer to our economic crisis. He had tried his hand at many money-making enterprises before finally specializing in an agricultural operation. At the age of fourteen he had successfully negotiated a monopoly position in respect of the horses' manure from the local coal merchants and dairies. With the enthusiasm of an empire-builder he granted fifty per cent of the profits to other boys to whom he sub-contracted the work of collection and delivery. Johnny looked after sales and was alleged to be netting more income than his father.

'Some of my boys are making over a pound a week,' he said expansively. When I didn't comment he knew Maurice and I had no aspirations in his particular field.

'Papers are fetching around five shillings a week,' Johnny said, referring to newspaper deliveries. This again was not practicable. Apart from any other consideration there was no question of our being in business on Saturdays.

'Car-washing is no good,' I volunteered unnecessarily. Every car-owner we knew washed his own car or had a professional job done at a local garage.

'I know a man who pays fivepence a hundred for addressing envelopes, if you're interested,' Johnny offered, 'but it will cost you a penny return to get to him.'

It seemed an odd price to pay and the travelling time and the fares made the offer unattractive.

'Why fivepence?' I asked, purely out of curiosity.

'Well,' my class-mate began slowly, 'he actually pays six-

The Munich Crisis

pence, but I charge a penny a hundred for the introduction.'

I said nothing. Johnny Stone was the first of a long line of businessmen I was to meet who demanded a commission from any commercial introduction, however trivial. 'It's not much of a deal,' I said.

'Cigarette cards pay less,' he said thoughtfully. 'You wouldn't like errand rounds or van-loading and there's not much else these days.'

When I left Johnny's house I walked slowly to the local park. I didn't want to return home and confess to Maurice that Johnny hadn't produced one practical suggestion. I had often spoken about the business mogul of our class and, quite unreasonably, I felt let down.

My wandering thoughts about pocket-money and jobs and other temporary problems were mingled with the certainty that things would come right.

I just felt a little lonely that I could not think of one person with whom I could discuss our financial affairs, who would not think we were trying to cadge. Walking round the lake for the second time, I heard a man call from the boat-house.

'Have you a moment, son?'

A few minutes later I was helping him to row his canoes into the centre of the lake. We took five out, tied them up and then rowed another back to the bank. This exercise was repeated for over an hour, during which time the man and I exchanged opinions on most of the important problems in the world.

When I walked home from the park I could feel several blisters forming on my hands, but the happy sense of achievement was out of all proportion to the shilling which my labours had earned. Maurice became my partner in the boat security exercise. No fortunes were made but our earnings enabled us to buy birthday presents for most of the family for the next few months and there was no need to compound father's problems with requests for more pocket-money.

The following year, our friend Bob Watson, who ran the

canoe house, took his motor-boat to Dunkirk. One of the five British soldiers he rescued from the Channel was Johnny Stone's brother.

XVI

Loose Connection

By any normal standards, my family could not claim to have been well connected in the fields of politics or commerce. However, from a very early age I had no doubt whatever that both my parents had inherited considerable influence with the Almighty. It was never actually said, but we children firmly believed that when it came to celestial powers, our family had direct lines of communication which had been established and enjoyed for generations.

'Prayers open the gates of heaven,' my mother would say with conviction. 'The Almighty is our greatest Protector, who sees everything we do and hears everything we say,' she would tell us regularly. For some time this last statement forced us to keep many of our thoughts to ourselves. Eventually, my brother Maurice and I decided that there was a fair chance that distance was on our side and, if we kept our voices down, our conversation might not reach the threshold of Paradise.

'Have you prayed this morning?' Maurice asked, one day.

'Yes, of course,' I said in my usual pitch.

'Did you say everything?' He persisted a little more quietly.

'No,' I whispered.

'Nor me,' he said, and then, very faintly, 'What do you think will happen?'

I didn't like the question, but I knew I had to say something. 'I don't know,' I replied in a hush. 'But Mama said that God forgives all sinners, so maybe we'll get away with it.'

'I'm not sinning yet,' Maurice said aggressively. 'I'm just not saying all the prayers, that's all.' He looked down at his feet and, before I could say anything, he asked, 'Have you got any new prayers?'

'Yes,' I said, confidentially. 'Only one.' I shook my head. 'But it's not working. I keep praying for Mr Bray' (who was our French teacher) 'to get a better job.'

Maurice thought about this for a moment and then observed, 'Maybe you're making it too difficult. Why not just another job?'

'I wanted to keep it like a nice prayer,' I said thoughtfully.

My brother didn't pursue this particular supplication as he was seriously concerned with one of his own.

'Have you ever prayed for more pocket-money?' he whispered. This ingenious idea of my nine-year-old brother had never occurred to me.

'No,' I said honestly. 'Have you?'

'Not yet,' he said. 'I just didn't want to ask for too much. . . .'

'Too much!' I repeated enthusiastically, not allowing him to finish his sentence. 'Too much! When you think of all those miracles He performed so easily, a bit of extra pocket-money . . .' I stopped suddenly as I caught sight of my mother standing in the doorway of our bedroom. She was smiling, but we didn't know how long she'd been standing there.

'You boys should be out playing in the lovely sunshine,' she said, but she was really telling us that God had given us good health and a lovely garden.

The pocket-money prayer occupied my thoughts for several days. The idea had enormous appeal, but I was consciously hesitant to ask God directly for money. I wondered if Maurice might ask for both of us and I would pray for something for him.

'After all,' I put the case to him later, 'we do want Him to listen and maybe it's better if one of us does the talking.'

'Praying's private,' Maurice said as though I was trespassing on his act and expecting half the profits.

Quite suddenly, I had the answer. 'We shouldn't ask for money,' I said a little pompously. 'We should pray for something to give to somebody else which we need money for. That's a proper prayer, isn't it?'

Maurice pondered on this for a while and then announced his decision. 'I don't think you can fool God,' he said with deliberation. 'I'm going to pray for money!'

The next morning as we walked to school, we compared notes.

'Did you pray for IT?' he asked in a whisper, not wishing to be overheard by the Deity.

'In a way, yes,' I answered. 'I prayed for all the usual things and then prayed that I should worry less about pocket-money, which I was sure I would if I had a bit more of it.'

'It won't work,' Maurice said authoritatively. 'That's not a good prayer.'

He was proved absolutely right. Our level of pocket-money remained unchanged. Despite this fact, there was no question of either of us losing faith. We knew that there was a great deal to be thankful for and remained convinced that many of our prayers were answered. After all, our parents continued to survive as our parents and provide us with enough to eat, at a time when the world was full of orphaned children and hungry people.

A short while after I attempted to bring the attention of Providence to my precarious financial position, my mother announced a miracle. 'God is truly merciful,' he said. 'Mrs Hart's completely cured, after being crippled with arthritis for six years.'

'Which Mrs Hart?' I asked.

'The poor woman with the two sticks, who took half an hour to walk to the corner. You remember how she used to walk!' my mother exclaimed. 'It's truly a miracle.'

'Has she got a new doctor?' Maurice asked.

Silence invaded the room to give my mother time to recover

her position with dignity and conviction.

'Yes,' she replied honestly. 'But the doctor could never have cured her without the Almighty's help'.

Maurice frowned and gripped his chin. 'Was her old doctor a sinner?' he asked.

My mother never failed to evade this sort of question and still leave us with the firm belief that the Almighty was fully employed working in the interests of our family and other privileged gentlefolk.

Later, when we were alone, Maurice made no direct reference to the miracle in our road. He simply confided to me that he had stopped praying for money.

Some three years after this incident, my complacent attitude to our halcyon approach to prayer was violently shattered. If the celestial portals really opened to the entreaties of our family, I felt, this was the time to prove it.

'Maurice,' I said, very seriously one evening, when he was twelve and I was fourteen. 'We better pray for Daddy, he's very ill.'

'I'm praying,' he said. Then, very softly, 'Will he get better?'

'He must get better,' I said positively, but secretly I was afraid he wouldn't.

'Can we ask other people to pray too?' Maurice suggested.

'You could,' I answered, 'but I expect God to listen to *us*.' As far as I was concerned, the Almighty knew our family better than most and it didn't seem right that we should have to recruit outside assistance.

Maurice and I said our prayers several times a day after that. We didn't pray for pocket-money, or for personal possessions, or for anybody else. We just prayed for our father. If the doctors wanted to help, that was fine with us, but we were relying on prayer.

A few weeks later, Father died. As I walked away from his grave, I looked through the rain up at the sky and I knew that my relationship with the Almighty would never be the same. If He was responsible for the celestial statistics, then He had got it wrong and there was a case for serious prayer to be temporarily suspended. Rotating in my mind was the quotation, 'And the wicked shall be punished, sayeth the Prophet,' and I knew that Mother and us kids were innocent. The mechanism that helped me swallow the lump in my throat was working overtime and I held back my tears. I was barely fifteen and I felt that my youth was already over.

As is customary, Mother, Esther, Sonnie, Maurice and I sat on low chairs and mourned Father for seven days. Judith and Leonard were considered too young to mourn with us and they were looked after by relations in the country. During that week, there was a constant flow of old friends and relations who called to express their sympathy and tell us what a wonderful father we had lost. Their well-meaning eulogies brought no comfort to Maurice or me. Some of the visitors were so clumsy in their choice of words that we would have laughed aloud had we not felt so hurt.

By the end of that week I had resumed praying, but without the same enthusiasm. During the period of mourning, various rabbis had emphasized the importance of praying for departed souls. Having failed miserably in my Divine negotiations with the Almighty on behalf of Father, I had no faith left for this extension of the exercise.

When the crunch came to start sorting ourselves out, it was Uncle Julius who was always there to help us. His own financial resources were very limited, but he gave us more than we were entitled to expect. He had only recently married an extremely attractive girl and his constant concern for our welfare was a further reflection of his wonderful nature.

Despite all the financial, emotional and social problems which hit our family through Father's death, Mother was determined that we should continue with our studies.

'You will both go back to school and we will manage,' she told

Maurice and me. This was not the time to argue with her, but later that evening we discussed the position in our room.

'I am going out to work,' I said positively.

Maurice had spoken very little for days, but he had also controlled his tears. 'What about Sonnie?' he asked, not really knowing the financial position of our eldest brother. In fact he was studying for a rabbinical diploma and his income, from teaching, was very modest.

'He'll do everything he can,' I said, without realizing the enormous responsibility Sonnie was going to accept for several years ahead.

In reality Maurice and I were emotionally and spiritually drained during the early days after our loss. We were not in a position to think straight or to plan and neither of us could have anticipated the journey which was just ahead of us.

XVII
My Uncle Harry

When Maurice and I travelled by train from London to Newcastle, railways still operated the three-class system. One had to be hard up and unspoilt to enjoy travelling third, on a long journey, and we qualified on both counts.

My father had died only two weeks previously and several of his old friends had sworn, on all that was holy, that we would never be in need so long as there was blood in their veins. These oaths simply proved to us that man can live without blood. It also left my mother, with six children, wondering what to do after she had exhausted Father's overdraft. At this sensitive time, she was persuaded by a misguided relative that it would be appropriate for Maurice and me to spend some time at a Yeshiva. This was a perfect example of excessive zeal tempered with immature judgement.

'I want to be a doctor,' Maurice said, as though we had all forgotten his ambition.

'I don't know what I want to be,' I told him, 'but I'm not interested in this sort of college.'

Despite some resentment and many misgivings, we were quietly excited at the prospect of travelling into the unknown. 'Did you ever think anybody would have any idea like this?' I asked Maurice, when we were seated comfortably in the train.

'I'm not thinking about it now,' he answered. 'If we don't like it, we don't stay, do we?' Maurice remarked to himself.

'And what happens if we do like it?' He looked at me sideways and shook his head. 'It won't happen,' he said, 'I can tell.'

We ate our sandwiches slowly and spent most of the time looking out of the windows. We both checked the price of lemonade and, learning that it cost a penny for a small cup, decided to do without it. We were not actually unhappy, we were just wistful. Neither of us had any idea what to expect at our destination and it seemed pointless speculating.

'You never really objected,' Maurice said suddenly, in an aggrieved voice.

'It wasn't the right time,' was all I could think of saying.

'I bet you we'll be home sooner than they expect,' he answered with determination.

At Newcastle Station we were approached by a short man with a twinkling smile and a ginger Vandyke beard. He was my late father's only brother, Uncle Harry. We had never met him before. 'You boys must be hungry,' were his first words and he immediately endeared himself to us. 'Your aunt has prepared a fine supper for you,' he added, as we walked towards the oldest tram I had ever seen.

The time that we spent in the north of England could be more accurately described as a traumatic experience than a spiritual happening or an educational excercise. But certain incidents remain permanently inscribed on my memory.

Uncle Harry was a devoutly religious man who attended the synagogue three times a day and managed to earn a modest living. Each morning when he re-entered his house he would leave his front door open and it would stay open until he went to bed.

'Why don't you lock your door?' Maurice asked him one day.

He looked at my brother, obviously surprised at the question, and said quietly. 'If a poor man comes to my house, I do not want to embarrass him by making him knock at my door.'

'What if he's a thief?' I asked.

Uncle Harry smiled. 'There's nothing here to steal,' he said.

Frequently, when we dined with him, a stranger would appear at the door of the dining-room. My uncle would immediately jump up and welcome him like an old friend. 'I've been hoping you would come,' he would invariably say, and gently lead the man to a seat, next to him, at the top of the table. My aunt always laid an extra place in case such a guest arrived. It was a custom of their house.

'I love having an intelligent man to talk to,' my uncle would say, as though the beggar was doing him a good turn. 'One meets so few interesting people these days,' he would often start, leading his guest to choose his own conversation.

'He's a great host,' Maurice whispered to me one evening, when Uncle Harry was entertaining a semi-literate pauper. 'That poor chap will think he's a relation soon.'

We both wondered whether, in fact, this particular visitor was a regular and, when he left, I asked my uncle if he knew him.

'I don't know him,' he replied. 'He's just a poor man who needed a meal and happened to find my door open.' He winked when he said it, but never referred to it again.

The following Thursday I returned from the Yeshiva to find my uncle on the telephone. He beckoned me to sit down as he started speaking with a sense of great urgency. 'Whatever you can lend me, I'll be grateful,' he said, 'I promise to pay it back but I cannot tell you when.'

This was the pattern of his conversation as he telephoned one person after another. 'I'm sorry,' he said to several people, 'I do have to have it today. It's a pretty desperate situation and tomorrow could be too late.' After each call he made a little note on a large piece of paper. 'I think I've got what I need,' he said to me at last.

I followed him out of the house and for nearly two hours we walked from house to house, collecting odd amounts of from five to twenty pounds. He did not spend any time chatting or explaining. He simply took the money, shook hands with the lender and walked off. Eventually, we boarded a tram to Newcastle where I followed my uncle into a furniture store. Within a few moments he had counted out most of the money, obtained a receipt and we were back on the pavement again. Standing at the side of the kerb was an enormous furniture van.

'You get the tram, mate, and we'll follow it,' the driver called out to my uncle.

It took us several hours to help unload the van and furnish three small houses on the outskirts of Newcastle.

'Do all customers help the drivers in these parts?' I asked my uncle.

'No,' he answered, and I heard him laugh for the first time that day. 'We're helping because we're saving money this way.' He didn't explain any further and I didn't ask him to.

We were just about to start our journey home when a white van arrived. The driver had called to deliver large parcels of groceries and fruit to each house and, again, my uncle and I helped. The man was paid there and then from the balance of the money which we had collected earlier.

It was not until the following morning that I discovered what the exercise was all about. We had just finished breakfast when the telephone rang.

'You can connect from midday,' my uncle said. 'That was the electricity company,' he explained.

That May morning, one of the last refugee boats from Holland arrived at the docks in Newcastle. My Uncle Harry simply approached three families whom he had never seen before, and in English or Yiddish, he told them that they were expected. Together, we escorted them to their new homes and my uncle spent the next two hours explaining their new surroundings to them. Before we left, a representative of the local refugee society arrived to take over.

'Do you know any of them?' I asked him, as we walked down the road.

'I know they're refugees,' he said. 'I don't need to know

anything else about them.'

'But why didn't you tell some of the people who lent you the money?' I queried.

'It would have taken too long,' he answered. Then very wearily, he added, 'And they would have wanted to know so many things which I don't need to know.'

It took my uncle ten years to repay the last instalment of the loans. Two weeks later, he died.

I remain grateful to him for this memory.

XVIII
Apprenticeship

We had been in the north of England for just over a month when the emotion-packed letters from my mother began to arrive without money orders. The sad message was all too clear to Maurice and me. Spiritually and psychologically she was right behind us, but financially, we were on our own.

'Do you think she needs help?' was Maurice's first reaction.

'I doubt it,' I said, simply to reassure him.

Maurice was obviously very concerned about the ramifications of our new position. 'What about us?' he asked, knowing precisely how little we had.

'Don't worry, we'll find some work,' I answered without hesitation.

He gave me his sideways look, stuck out his chin and nodded his head. 'We can't really afford to be broke at the moment,' he said soulfully.

Uncle Harry, who must have known or suspected our financial strength, offered to give us the small allowance we had been receiving.

'We're not really short, yet,' Maurice assured him.

'Well,' my uncle began, but I didn't let him finish his sentence.

'If we need anything, we'll certainly ask you, Uncle.'

That evening we discussed our independent attitude and decided that we had to take the initiative, very quickly, if we were to retain our pride.

Apprenticeship

At the first opportunity, we went to see the only businessman we knew, Mr Hart, the baker. He was a kind man who worked very long hours in a shop which was invariably untidy. We were confident that there was money to be earned clearing it up for him.

'Boys,' he said, shaking his head regretfully, 'I really can't offer you anything. You see,' he explained, 'my brother does the baking, my wife and I look after the shop and my sister-in-law does the books.'

'Who cleans the place?' Maurice asked hopefully. Mr Hart smiled at him.

'A good question,' he said, looking round the shop. 'We all try to keep the place clean and sometimes, even my mother helps.'

We guessed that he was trying to tell us that he didn't have any money to pay anybody, even if there was work to be done. It was obvious that Mr Hart had a difficult time making a living from the three classes of customer who patronized him. There were those who bought fresh bread and cakes, others who bought everything, at a discount, when it was two days old, and then there was the Theological College cook who bought what was left over.

'I really wish I could do something for you,' Mr Hart said, 'and if I hear of anybody, I'll let you know.' The poor man looked very tired and Maurice and I felt so sorry for him, we spent that afternoon cleaning his shop for nothing.

'May God bless you,' he intoned when we were leaving and handed us a bag of his two-day-old raisin buns.

'We'll help you again,' Maurice told him politely. We never did, because Mr Hart solved our problem far sooner than we imagined.

Only two days later he introduced us to a well-known character in the town, Mr Max Romer, who offered us a part-time job. He was a tall man with black, smiling eyes and a full patriarchal beard. He was a widower with five grown-up daughters, each one of whom was long on culture and short on glamour. Mr Romer was under no illusions regarding their matrimonial potential and employed a specialist to help him with his problem. This connoisseur, whose name was Fischer, had a long, successful track record with cases which required expert presentation.

'Nothing is impossible, given time,' Fischer would say with conviction.

Mr Romer studied us very carefully. 'You boys can collect some of the rents,' he opened pleasantly. 'My business,' he continued, 'is to manage several hundred little houses for their owners. One client owns nearly three streets of them and they could be a good start for you.'

'How much do we get paid?' I asked.

He smiled and nodded approval at my question. 'Well,' he started slowly. 'Let us say, you each get three shillings for the Durham Estate if you make a good job of it.'

On the way out, one of the daughters, Annie, gave Maurice a bag of fruit. 'And what's your favourite meal?' she enquired kindly.

'Eggs and chips,' we replied enthusiastically.

Annie Romer was one of the few women I ever met who looked plain when she smiled and quite stupid when she laughed.

'She'll need more than Mr Fischer to help her,' Maurice said later.

The following afternoon, after attending the Yeshiva, we travelled by tram for nearly one hour and then walked a further mile to Durham Road. We were very shaken when we arrived. The rows of three-storey miners' dwellings were the most primitive we had ever seen and the wooden toilet cubicles that lined the yards explained the rents.

'No wonder they only pay three shillings and sixpence a week,' Maurice said.

I remember clearly that it began to rain as we approached the door of number 1a Durham Road. We collected the rent, signed the rent book and placed a tick beside the address on our record sheet.

'That wasn't difficult,' I said happily. 'At this rate we can finish the job in about three hours.'

'That would put us on lower wages than a charlady,' Maurice said factually, without resentment.

In reality, we both spoke too soon. At the next little home, perched on a second floor, the door was slammed in our faces. 'No rent this week,' an untidy woman screamed at us, and we were left standing, on a fire escape, in a state of suspended shock.

'Maybe she's ill,' Maurice suggested.

'Maybe she has no money,' I said, thinking it more likely.

We received this treatment from four of our next ten calls and we both knew that we were completely out of our depth in coping with the situation. We sat on a low brick wall wondering whether or not to admit failure, when a tall, middle-aged man approached us. He was shabbily dressed, had a black patch over one eye and smelt heavily of beer and tobacco. 'You lads got problems?' he asked. He had a strange, kind voice and within a short while we had told him our sad story.

'Come with me,' he said firmly. 'I'll show 'em.'

He only told us that his name was Jim and that he knew every family in the neighbourhood. We revisited the door-slammers and, in each case, Jim told the same story. 'These lads aren't just rent collectors,' he shouted. 'They're orphans and,' he exaggerated, 'if they go back without your rent, they starve and their brother and sister starve with 'em.'

Until that moment we had never thought of ourselves as orphans and we were quite stunned by the thought. Without hesitation, each tenant, prompted by Jim, paid the rent and, to our embarrassment, many of them gave us cake and sweets. Later we learned that Jim had lost his eye rescuing ten men in a pit disaster and this had made him a hero among his mates and their families. He stayed with us until we had visited every tenant, and then wrote down his address in case we should have any trouble in the future. None of us could have anticipated the circumstances in which we were to meet again.

It was after ten that night, when we returned to the house of Mr Romer. He and Mr Fischer were marching up and down the small lounge when we entered. They both stopped and stared. 'What happened?' they asked together. 'Where have you been?' Apparently we were at least three hours later than they expected and they had obviously been very worried.

'It took much longer . . . ' I began apologetically.

'How many people didn't pay?' Mr Romer asked, quickly becoming practical.

'Only one lady,' Maurice said.

The men stared at one another and then at us. 'One?' shouted Mr Romer in a tone of disbelief. 'Everybody else paid?' he said in amazement.

We quietly preened ourselves on our achievement and didn't mention our new friend.

That evening, Annie Romer made us a large plate of eggs and chips. 'Father is very pleased with you, boys,' she said, giving us one of her unique smiles, which made us feel pity for her.

When we returned to the drawing-room to say goodnight and collect our wages, Mr Romer was holding a large photo of a young man in front of him. The young man had a bald head, thick glasses and a large mouth.

'Fischer,' he said soulfully, raising the palm of his free hand towards the ceiling, 'so my Annie is no oil painting, so this young man comes from a good family, but have you thought what my grand-children would look like?'

It was after midnight when we left the house with our first wages.

'Those people in Durham Road are tough,' I said, as we were going to sleep.

'They must love orphans,' Maurice said drowsily.

Apprenticeship

The tenants on the estate continued to pay their rent promptly and Mr Romer soon raised our wages by sixpence a week. This enabled us to start saving for our escape from the Yeshiva, which had been our ambition ever since we had arrived.

Whenever we appeared at the home of Max Romer, two things were certain. Mr Fisher would be there discussing marriage-broking, and Annie would make us eggs.

'So-o-o-o, Fischer,' began Mr Romer one day, 'and what became of the wonderful Mr Harris from London?' and he then ran together a long scale of M's to make a question, rather like 'MMMMMMMMM?'

'I was actually too late,' confessed Fischer, clasping his hands.

'Too late, Fischer?' Mr Romer asked with surprise. 'With your experience, you let a bridegroom like Mr Harris get married without you?'

Fischer smiled and went through the procrastinating process of clapping and clasping his hands. 'Mr Harris did not get married,' he announced in self-defence. 'He let it be known that he has become a philosopher and he is not including marriage in his programme.'

'So-o-o-o-o,' beamed Mr Romer, like a man who has just solved a difficult problem. 'Tell our young philosopher that, according to Plato, Life is a lottery.'

'I thought of that,' Fishcer said, 'but Harris told me that he wasn't a gambler!'

Mr Romer nodded his head many times before commenting. 'With answers like that,' he started, 'maybe it's better he stays single. Aggravation I have enough without such philosophers in my family.'

Some weeks later we had nearly completed our round of rent collecting when we heard the roar of men's voices pouring down Durham Road. At first, fear and horror registered on the faces of all the wives and elderly people who emerged from their homes. Each expression screamed, 'pit disaster' for several seconds, until it became clear that the men were singing, not shouting. Maurice and I were swept along with the dozens of people who rushed to meet the men from the pits.

'The war can't be over yet,' Maurice said.

'Maybe they got more pay,' I offered.

We soon learned that the men were singing with pride bcause one hundred of the boys from their pits had been allowed to enlist in the local regiment. When we joined them, the men were kissing their wives and sweethearts and slapping each other on their backs. We were very soon included in the celebrations, as were the local publicans, who rolled out several barrels of beer on to the pavements for the occasion.

'You've got to be very happy or unhappy to enjoy this stuff,' Maurice said, drinking beer for the first time.

'We're proud of our boys,' somebody shouted.

'The war will soon be over now,' boasted another.

'I wouldn't be a German soldier now my Tom's joined up,' laughed a woman who had swilled beer down her apron.

From the sheltered background of our home and the Yeshiva, my brother and I were being introduced to a new side of life and indeed a new vocabulary.

Eventually, we all formed an enormous circle and sang 'Rule Britannia'. Then the party broke up and everybody began to make their way home.

'We better run for the tram,' I said, realizing that we were very late. But Maurice hadn't heard me. He had walked over to inspect a drunk who was holding desperately on to a gas-lit lamp-post.

'It's Jim,' he shouted as though he were a survivor from a shipwreck. 'He'll never stand up by himself,' he said pityingly. We had kept his address at the back of our note-book and together we dragged Jim to his home. It took us nearly an hour to cover a few hundred yards.

'He'll want to thank you boys personally,' his wife said proudly, when we brought him through the door.

Apprenticeship

'He doesn't owe us anything,' we assured her, but she didn't know what we were talking about.

It was very late when we returned to Mr Romer. 'Have you been in a fight, heaven forbid?' he greeted us. It was then that we realized that we must be covered in soot from the miners, who had not washed before we joined their party. We also remembered that we had rushed off without collecting rent from eight of the tenants.

'You'll have to go back tomorrow,' Mr Romer said. 'By next week they will have spent it and,' he added, pointing a waving forefinger at us, 'you will have to pay the fare yourselves. That's what business is about,' he added in explanation.

'Tell them I found a bridegroom for your Tilly,' Fischer called from the other side of the small room.

Mr Max Romer smiled broadly and his bright eyes shone. 'It's perfectly true,' he conceded. 'Fischer has another success story. Maybe not a bargain, but a bridegroom, he's found.'

We didn't wait for the chips that evening because we were afraid that Annie might smell that we had drunk beer. It had been an eventful day which we discussed long into the night. 'I suppose it's fair to send us back to the estate,' I said as we were going to sleep.

'It's not easy money, is it?' Maurice posed the question to the small, dark room.

The following day, the evacuation from Dunkirk began.

It was a coincidence that on that day we should also decide to leave this bastion of ultra-orthodoxy in the north of England. This was no reflection on the sincerity of these pious pedagogues who devoted their lives to teaching the customs and laws of the Faith. They believed in the infallibility of the Bible and its commentators and allowed no margin for secular education. This limited intellectual approach was quite foreign to our upbringing and extremely difficult to accept. It appeared incongruous that, at a time when millions of Jews were heading towards the gas-chambers, our teachers should be basking in the glory of the miracles performed in Sinai.

There were few miracles around in Europe at that time and Maurice and I reckoned that if Providence was still interested in mankind, this was a good time for a repeat performance. Neither of us had the courage to express these blasphemous views, but we did not share the religious fervour of our mentors. Still, we were not unduly impetuous. We did not wish to offend Uncle Harry, so we did not discuss our proposed exodus with him. Knowing the financial straits that Mother was struggling through, we saw no point in adding to her troubles. Our only hope was to find enough part-time work to earn the fare back to London.

The rigid discipline of the Yeshiva made our task infinitely more difficult than we had, at first, appreciated. We would get up at six-thirty every morning in order to attend the early service. This was followed, an hour later by breakfast, which invariably consisted of dry bread and mugs of tea. There was relatively little time for this meal as we ate at tables which had to be cleared for our first lessons, starting at eight o'clock.

Most of each day was taken up studying the Bible, the Talmud and Commentaries. At no time did doubt ever creep into any discussion other than to question the difference between the opinions of rabbis who might well have lived in the first or second centuries. We studied the ancient laws of property and indemnity; of justice and of litigation; of marriage and dignity, and it was readily acknowledged that the laws of most civilized nations were based on these precepts.

We studied with a certain sense of pride, but without complete conviction. We acknowledged the wisdom but questioned its origin. We respected our rabbis, but suspected their limitations. We appreciated the unflinching zeal, but missed the flexibility of thought. We admired the resolution of purpose and acceptance of Divine guidance, but Maurice and I knew we were in transit.

This centre of theology might have lacked the intellectual dimension of a twentieth-century university, but it certainly projected a spiritual charisma out of all proportion to its size. The daily lectures on behaviour and ethics indoctrinated a level of courtesy and integrity which would have embellished any university syllabus. The sages of old would have blessed this establishment and the ancient guardians of our heritage might well have found refuge within its walls, but Maurice and I were two generations too late. Our orthodox upbringing had been tempered with a secular education, and though we could accept that God created man in His own image, we doubted man's right to return the compliment. If these old barracks housed the army of the Lord, we were unworthy recruits.

Our decision to leave this Yeshiva did not require any great heart-searching, but implementing it was to prove more difficult. Our wages from Max Romer were too erratic to enable us to plan our exodus within a reasonable time. Although he was an amusing and hospitable character, our pay was invariably less than we expected, and we were obliged to calculate the following week's income to balance our budget. It was quite apparent that we had to find an additional or alternative source of income within the limited leisure time available.

All students who enrolled at the Yeshiva were obliged to study from eight in the morning until six in the evening, but the majority of students continued their Talmudic discourses until much later into the night. The piety of those who opted out after ten hours a day was definitely suspect. Maurice and I fell into this latter category, which provided further proof that our zeal was lacking for this particular brand of scholarship. The only light relief was alternate Wednesday afternoons when students were permitted to deal with personal matters, or discuss the text they were studying, in the park. We decided that this was the time to look for odd jobs to pay our fare back to a society to which we felt more attuned. The life-style of the Yeshiva might well have been unique in the Western world, but our personal chemistry was obviously unsuited for this form of evangelizing within the Faith.

On the first free Wednesday afternoon, Maurice found a job

addressing envelopes — by hand, of course. It had few possibilities in terms of entrepreneurial potential, but the pay was 6d a hundred envelopes and there was no shortage of work at that rate. Allowing for errors and travelling expenses, an afternoon's work produced about 2/6. I called on over forty shop-keepers without any success. It was quite understandable that hard-working northern tradesmen were not impressed by a fifteen-year-old boy who offered to work up to three hours a week. My genuine enthusiasm for limited employment made little impression and these potential employers mostly offered me the door even before I had finished my verbal application. My vocabulary of expletives was certainly enriched by these gentlemen, but the experience definitely undermined my self-confidence.

On the tram back to Gateshead a man asked me for a cigarette but I was unable to help him.

'There ain't much work in North,' he said discouragingly. I nodded in sympathy, as my feet were already sending me the same message.

'Do you manage to get a few odd jobs?' I asked, hoping for a useful tip from a fellow-sufferer. His expression carried a look bordering on disbelief.

'People do odd jobs theyselves in North,' he mumbled with the air of a master addressing a greenhorn. Silenced by this answer I watched the man move down the length of the tram in search of a cigarette. The fourth man he approached gave him a Woodbine. He broke it in two, placing one half in his mouth and the other in an empty tin box which had long ago contained medicinal tablets. He struck a match on the sole of his shoe, and, with his free hand, protected the flame all the way to the half-cigarette. My concentration was interrupted by the tram conductor who had obviously overheard my conversation.

'You might get some Saturday work in the town, if you keep trying,' he offered helpfully. I smiled as politely as I could, knowing it was quite impossible to explain to this well-wisher

Apprenticeship

the implications of being a Yeshiva student.

During the succeeding days I relived the interviews countless times trying to understand why I had consistently failed to generate a spark of interest in so many shopkeepers. High unemployment, keen competition and small profit margins were all excuses rather than reasons which I could accept and I was determined to keep trying.

'Do you want to address envelopes?' Maurice asked, offering to use his influence on my behalf. The gesture was typically generous but I was determined to find my own job.

Constantly recalling memories of my humiliating experiences prevented me from concentrating on my Talmudic studies. My wandering mind carried me backwards and forwards to different local shopping parades and to imaginary interviews which I conducted with enormous aplomb.

'If an ox gores a cow,' said my teacher, in Hebrew, 'what are the legal implications?' The question failed to break through my daydream, which was working overtime with successful Newcastle businessmen.

Maurice's foot brought me back to reality, but by that time the question had been readdressed to him. In keeping with the way we had been taught the answer was presented in the following form: 'It depends if the cow was in calf. Also it is necessary to know if the cow was on its owner's land or was trespassing. Furthermore,' continued Maurice, translating from the vernacular, 'one must consider if the owner of the ox was aware that it was a gorer and whether the owner of the cow had previously been warned of the danger.'

Not to appear as distracted as I really was, I joined the discussion by referring to a well-known commentary. 'Compensation might also be affected if the ox owner had only recently purchased the ox. In such circumstances one should question whether he was warned that the ox was a gorer.'

This debate was typical of the type of discourse which had been encouraged in similar institutions for over two thousand years. It would be interesting to analyse what other nations of the world were doing when the rabbis of old were interpreting the laws of compensation as laid down in the Torah. The purpose of our studying these legal processes was not in anticipation of our qualifying in agricultural law, but simply to teach us to think and to understand the many factors which must be taken into account in order to judge fairly. This form of study was both fascinating and enlightening, but we lacked the enthusiasm and the stoicism to persevere conscientiously for ten hours a day. The only other student who appeared to share our detachment was an older boy named Imre Hess. We never really became acquainted, but many years later I heard that he became an eminent brain surgeon in Florida.

The following Wednesday morning the Head of the Yeshiva delivered a two-hour homily on the significance of the hereafter. His profound dissertation continually made reference to the insignificance of earthly assets compared with celestial rewards. These honours, he repeatedly emphasized, were directly related to our behaviour on earth and our observance of the major and minor commandments. He was genuinely convinced that the glory of such recognition would serve as adequate incentive even to the less pious who had infiltrated these walls. As always, it was an impressive performance which we did not take personally. There was no doubt that this emotional oration encouraged the more devout solemnly to calculate the likely rates of exchange between this world and the next. Nobody actually discussed the principles of good-deed scoring, but the concept of a celestial *bourse* operating convertible currency had enormous potential for exploitation.

'I think I'm too young to be judged on such a grand scale,' Maurice said, reflecting my own thoughts. We were concerned about earning our fares back to London and could not afford the luxury of such long-range planning. If this was to prejudice our priority on the road to the Millennium, we trusted that the

Almighty, in his mercy, would grant us some dispensation. Listening diligently to an inspired formula for salvation was an experience afforded to the privileged, but we did not feel an immediate commitment to experiment with the recipe.

'It was convincing when he was speaking . . . ' I started expounding to Maurice, who was wearing his favourite frown.

'He wasn't talking from first-hand experience,' Maurice interrupted, and we both laughed.

That afternoon Maurice went off to earn his shilling addressing envelopes and I made my way to Newcastle to further my search for part-time work. The confidence which I had developed during lessons quickly evaporated and the discouraging experiences of the previous week repeated themselves with monotonous regularity.

'I want to get to London,' I told one shopkeeper, hoping it might encourage him to give me a break. He seemed to find this amusing.

'It's overrated,' he said, and waved me off the premises.

I walked into a small tobacconist's and examined the thin, poker-faced owner who was sucking at a large empty pipe. His soiled white coat barely hid his woollen vest, and his dreamy blood-shot eyes advertised his intemperance. He did not have the appearance of a man anxious for an assistant. I made my usual application and before he could remove his pipe, I added, 'It could give you a chance to take your wife to the cinema or something.' His use of expletives was impressive if somewhat repetitive.

'I'm not looking for any help with my shop or my marriage,' he bellowed in rather unpoetic language.

'There's no trade here on Wednesdays,' said a fishmonger. 'Why not try the brick-yard?' This suggestion was the most constructive that I had been offered so far, but I decided to try it only as a last resort. I did not possess any overalls and I was reluctant to put my limited wardrobe at risk.

In an effort to economize I decided to walk back to Gateshead and seriously consider taking up Maurice's suggestion of addressing envelopes. I had not yet reached the point of despair, but there was no doubt that I was approaching it pretty rapidly. Once again I started rehearsing my interviews in the hope that I could recognize a reason for my failure. It was proving a fruitless exercise, but my thoughts were suddenly distracted by the sound of a man singing to the accompaniment of a banjo. He stood in the gutter with a card hanging round his neck declaring that he had tuberculosis and three children. I watched his Adam's apple work its way up and down his scraggy neck as he sang a ballad made famous in the First World War. I dropped a penny in his hat and walked on.

'You don't come from these parts,' the beggar said. I pondered on his words as I realized that I had just given away twenty-five per cent of my capital. On the other side of the road was an old man standing outside a second-hand bookshop. I crossed over to examine his penny-bargain stall.

'That was a nice thing to do, lad,' the old man said, referring to the incident he had obviously witnessed.

'He looks ill,' I said. The old man looked me up and down and invited me into his shop to examine his stock. Books of every description filled the room from floor to ceiling and the approach to the rear looked more like an obstacle race than a gangway.

'Do you have books at home?' the man asked. Those were the first really personal words I had heard since I began tramping the streets of Newcastle. Suddenly the dust and untidiness meant nothing. I was conscious of a man who lived with books and wanted to talk and was waiting for an answer to his question with a smile on his face. Unconsciously I had been waiting for someone to whom I could pour out my long tale of woe. I told him about my father's library and his love of Dickens and my mother's interest in international writers and how we had landed up in the Yeshiva in the next town and were desperate to get back to London.

Apprenticeship

'I've been looking for someone like you,' he said kindly, 'someone to help me tidy up these books.'

We both knew that it would need a great deal more than three hours a week to make any impression at all on this book mountain, but I accepted thankfully.

Edward Weller was the only Gentile among the friends I made during my stay in the North. He was a self-educated, kindly old man who showed the devotion to books that some over-protective women render only to their grandchildren. He agreed to pay me 1/- an hour plus fares and the promise of a bonus at the end of each month. When I left him after our first meeting he gave me 2/-.

'That's on account of your first bonus,' he said with a twinkle in his eye. 'I want to make sure you come back.' I left feeling happier than I had done for weeks and my confidence in the Almighty, in mankind and in myself was almost fully restored. I walked down the road to the bus-stop whistling the song the banjo-player had been singing. Meeting Ed Weller had been an exciting experience which I could hardly wait to relate to Maurice. But this pleasure was to be deferred for an unexpected reason which was to cause considerable embarrassment.

A few hundred yards from the bookshop I saw a youth of about eighteen standing over an upturned bicycle. 'Can yer give me a hand, mate?' he asked in a despondent tone. He was trying to repair a puncture with the aid of a knife and fork which he had borrowed from the railway. The delay was obviously causing him concern and I was pleased to hold the knife in position while he made another attempt to remove the tyre with the fork. Our joint effort resulted in his bending the fork in half and my drawing blood from three fingers, but the tyre remained firmly attached to the wheel.

'There's a junk-yard up the road,' he said, as though we had been partners for years. 'Pop up and see if you can find some sort of wheel.' Twenty minutes later I returned carrying an old buckled wheel which I had found on the dump. The reception I received seemed out of all proportion to the little trouble I had taken.

'They call me Chips,' the young man offered and then added, as though an explanation was necessary, 'I got the name because I peel spuds in the railway hotel.' This piece of information explained the origin of his working tools. He was far too intent on breaking some spokes from the bent wheel to acknowledge my name when I introduced myself.

'We'll have this right in a jiff,' he gasped and skilfully twisted the tin spokes round the bent fork so that it would hold the improvized tool in position. Having wrapped his red hankerchief round the knife, we made another attempt to remove the obstinate tyre. This time we succeeded and Chips's keen ear soon located the puncture. Fifteen minutes later he was cycling down the road yelling his appreciation over his shoulder.

Little did either of us imagine that we would meet again, three years later, on a troopship. When I recognized him then he said quickly, 'You look after me, mate, and I'll look after you.'

He had evidently exaggerated his position in civvy street and was trusting me to confirm his story if necessary. The occasion did not arise, but throughout the journey he made sure that I had adequate rations to compensate for the non-kosher meat which I did not eat. On the day the ship berthed, he handed me ten cigarettes. 'My Dad might'ave lost 'is job if I 'adn't got 'is bike 'ome in time,' he explained and walked away before I could thank him.

When I returned to our room at the Yeshiva, Maurice reminded me that it had been my turn to conduct the evening prayers and I was two hours late. I immediately reported to the Head and apologized.

'What happened to you?' he inquired with some concern.

There was no doubt that the true story would not have sounded plausible and in any case would have been quite unacceptable.

'I felt I wanted to be alone,' I said quietly. The old man stared at me for several seconds.

'Would you like to talk about your problems?' he asked kindly. It was a considerate suggestion, but one that I could hardly accept, any more than I could tell him that I found a confident in Ed Weller.

Now that our return home was nearer to reality, we used our lessons to help the time to pass rather than to question the wisdom of their substance. The Laws which related to reciting numerous Blessings each day were largely designed for man to acknowledge his gratitude to the Almighty. This fitted very well into our syllabus and helped us to appreciate the better aspects of our life. This was not too easy to accept, particularly when shoe repairs and haircuts diminished our hard-earned savings.

My job with Ed Weller was to sort the books into four catagories; sets, well-bound books in good condition, first editions and junk. They were nearly all sold to different sections of the trade, but Mr Weller was continually finding editions that he refused to part with. On my third visit, he told me that he had never known his parents, but the pictures of a Victorian couple on his wall depicted the parents he would have liked to have had.

'Sometimes I really believe I am their son,' he confided sadly after I had told him stories of my own parents. That day, I told him how we were expected to put in extra time at the Yeshiva in addition to the ten hours a day to which we were committed. He made no comment, but when I left his shop he handed me a book by Arnold Bennett called *How to Live on Twenty-Four Hours a Day*. 'It's worth reading every five years,' he said, nodding his head. I followed his suggestion for more than twenty years and would still recommend the book to anyone who believes the day is too short.

We had saved just over half the fares when a letter arrived from Mother telling us that our eldest sister, Esther, was getting married. Uncle Harry immediately offered to buy us return tickets and we were able to leave Gateshead without causing either offence or distress to anyone.

The Head of the Yeshiva never inquired when we were returning, but when we left he said, holding our hands together, 'Remember your duty to your fellow-man and you will not forget your duty to God.'

Those profound words were a little too deep for young boys in their early teens, but they have stayed with us throughout our lives. This Yeshiva may well have been narrow in its concept yet throughout the time we were there we never once heard words of envy, greed or scandal. To that extent, it remained unique among all the societies in which I was later to mix.

When I said good-bye to Ed Weller he gave me a bonus large enough to buy a wedding present for my sister.

We returned to Buckinghamshire where Mother and the rest of the family had been evacuated. Maurice was admitted to Amersham Grammar School where our youngest brother Leonard was already a pupil, and I started looking for a permanent job. The forthcoming family wedding was a cause of considerable excitement, but Mother was faced with the impossible task of finding the money to pay for a new wardrobe for Esther as well as a modest reception. The total required was in the region of £45; to see this figure in perspective, it represented twenty-five per cent of the annual salary of the average schoolmaster.

Burying her pride, my mother wrote to a number of old friends whom she justifiably imagined were in a positioin to make her a loan. Most never replied but one kind lady granted an interest-free loan of £50, only demanding the security of Mother's engagement ring. She deposited it without hesitation and without mentioning it to anyone. It is to the credit of my brother Sonnie that as soon as he learned of the story he started saving to redeem the pledge, and never bought any new clothes until he had done so.

Apprenticeship

Finding employment that did not require Saturday working proved extremely difficult as most businesses were open five and a half days a week. Eventually I found a job working for an evacuated burial society that required copies of all its records. For eight hours every day I would copy out the names, addresses and details of next-of-kin of the members of this august body. In the evenings I would either attend evening classes in mathematics and literature or receive further religious education.

My wages covered a little more than our rent and with Sonnie making the major contribution and my mother budgeting down to a penny, the pattern of a happy home began to emerge once again. Mother kept chickens and grew vegetables, became an ardent member of the local library and was still able to treat herself to her weekly literary paper. Each week brought news of another relation enlisting in the services. Several became chaplains, but two became RAF pilots and a cousin from Canada came over to join, and to die, with a Canadian tank regiment. Another cousin who was a professor of mathematics was commissioned in the Royal Engineers. It was the family's pride that they all volunteered and did not wait to be called up.

About this time I met Heinrich Eisemann, one of the foremost authorities on ancient books and manuscripts. A highly cultured, orthodox Jew, his immaculate, debonair appearance was more reminiscent of an international banker than a dealer in antiquarian books. His vast knowledge of religious and secular literature was acknowledged throughout the world and his willingness to share the fruits of his intelligence was matched only by his charm. Although I was younger than most of his children I had the good fortune to develop a rapport with him that was to last for more than twenty years. A measure of the esteem in which he was held was illustrated by the number of curators and other authorities who would stand when he entered a Sotheby's sale. Eminent rabbis, outstanding artists and men who had distinguished themselves in the fields of medicine, music and literature were numbered among his circle of close friends. It was through him that in later years I had the privilege of meeting Sir Adrian Boult, Jacob Epstein and the eminent surgeon, Dixon Wright. It was Heinrich Eisemann who encouraged me to read the work of Josephus, the Roman historian of the first century AD. As a result I became extremely interested in this period and those qualified to write about it, and the knowledge I acquired was, in some ways, complementary to what I had learned at the Yeshiva. The combination certainly proved invaluable when, a few years later, I studied the New Testament under the guidance of a Catholic priest.

The standard of teachers at the local evening classes was substantially higher than one would have expected from a small town in Buckinghamshire. This was largely due to the number of academics who had moved from London and found it necessary to augment their incomes. The only student with whom I became friendly was a young German refugee named Arthur Stilitz, who described himself as a lapsed Jew. His father had been a professor of physics in Vienna until the Nazis had marched him and his wife to a concentration camp. Stilitz had a great mathematical mind and considerable linguistic ability. His obsessive hate for the Germans was born more from the three-hundred-year history of his family in that country than from his identification with Judaism. In the second year of the war he underwent plastic surgery at the hands of McIndoe, changed his name and was parachuted into Berlin.

Twenty-five years later I met an old German priest who had retired to the Mount of Olives in Jerusalem. He swore that he had harboured Stilitz for several months before he joined the Nazi party in a determined effort to save Jews from the gas chambers. According to this priest, whom I had reason to believe, Stilitz returned to London after the war and became a director of a well-known merchant bank. I have never met him since the time we shared the same evening classes.

In those days Saturday continued to be the focal point of our

Apprenticeship

week. Although we all attended services on Friday evenings and Saturday mornings, we invariably had a variety of visitors for tea on Saturday afternoons. My Uncle Gabriel would frequently arrive for a game of chess with Maurice and spend time playing with the younger members of the family. A tall handsome man, he was very proud of having gone to Perse School and of being an old member of the Liberal Club. One day, Arthur Stilitz lost a game of chess to him after they had played for over an hour. Stilitz won the return game in five minutes and Uncle Gabriel never forgave himself for it. Although only twenty-two at that time, Stilitz was a person who was respected rather than liked. On one of the rare occasions that he visited our home he challenged Mother to recognize the different German dialects which he had perfected. She identified only four out of ten but she was extremely impressed with his performance.

Uncle Gabriel was an amusing popular member of the family and like the rest of our family and friends had an enormous regard for the intellect of Professor Sam Atlas, who was a frequent visitor. He was a lecturer in Comparative Religion and Ethics and his photographic memory enhanced his vast scholarship. 'The trouble with people who study is that they think they acquire wisdom,' he would say wittily.

It was always a worthwhile experience listening to Sam Atlas indulge in a controversial discussion with Professor David Dirringer, who occasionally visited us. He was one of the foremost authorities on Semitic epigraphy, a subject which he lectured at Cambridge. One of his best-known works was *The Alphabet: A Key to the History of Mankind*. Sam Atlas and David Dirringer were unusual men from different backgrounds, but each respected the wisdom of the other. Their quick-witted repartee was an intellectual game which was both entertaining and stimulating. We would frequently be joined by the Stamler brothers who, at that time, were both at school. Later Sam Stamler was to become an eminent QC and David succeeded

Kopul Rosen as headmaster of Carmel College. Their lively sense of humour further increased the pleasure of these happy occasions. The tea itself would consist of large quantities of tomato or jam sandwiches and plates of chocolate yeast cake which was Mother's speciality.

When I told Sam Atlas that I was reading Josephus he smiled. 'Remember he had a vested interest in a great deal of what he recorded.' This one sentence permanently affected my attitude to the writings of this Roman historian. Atlas emigrated to America, but Maurice and I have remained close friends with the Stamler brothers for nearly forty years.

The arm of coincidence has constantly touched my life and left me speculating on the course of many unpredictable events. In 1959 I visited Agadir, in Southern Morocco, on my honeymoon. The man to whom I carried a letter of introduction, from a senior RAF officer, had died a week before my arrival. Later I met his cousin, Albert Caucus, who was the son of the French officer who had been sent to raise the French flag over Agadir. He spoke perfect English which he claimed to have learned at Perse School in Cambridge. On the wall of his office was a photograph of all the students who attended the school at the same time. Seated in the front row was my uncle Gabriel. Sadly, Albert Caucus was to become a victim of the earthquake which destroyed most of Agadir the following year. His business was taken over by a French concern in Paris which later became associated with a London company of which I was a director.

Working alone in a one-roomed office, compiling records of members of a burial society, was more like serving a sentence than fulfilling an occupation. As an exercise in monotony I could think of no parallel, and I very soon realized that I had to create some form of relief. Halfway through each day I would feel that my mind was being anaesthetized by the uninspiring contribution I was making to the funeral industry. There was no possibility of changing my job as the fares to London would have eroded my wages and a five-day week in the locality was almost unheard of. After giving the matter considerable thought, I established that my employers were more than satisfied with the volume of work completed each week. It was therefore only necessary to practise writing more quickly and thereby complete the daily chore in a shorter number of hours. The promise of more reading-time encouraged me to accept this challenge with a determination which demanded both effort and discipline.

At the end of one month I had created a profit of over two hours' free time every day. It was during this period, over the next few months, that I became better acquainted with the works of Dostoevsky, Tolstoy and Descartes. As my book list grew, my working day began to have a purpose. Intermingled with Chekhov and Shakespeare, I would read Bates, Sinclair Lewis and Charteris. After a while I found that I could do my irksome job with little concentration and allow half my mind to speculate on imaginary conversations between such people as Omar Khayyám and Isaiah or Maimonides and Columbus.

This private hobby had so many possibilities that I was encouraged to widen my choice of literature in order to build a larger variety of real and fictitious characters. Each week the number of participants in my private debates and arguments increased and threw their philosophies and prejudices at one another with uninhibited enthusiasm. Each day I would choose those with whom I would share my seclusion. Chaucer might be confronted by Thomas Mann or Wilde would embarrass the Queen of Sheba in front of Neville Chamberlain. Mark Twain would ridicule Schopenhauer and Alice in Wonderland would discuss family problems with Noah.

Contrary to expectation these stimulating and controversial discussions gave my record writing even greater impetus and my limited work production increased noticeably. After four months I was given an unexpected increase in salary on account of my conscientiousness. During this period the characters of nearly fifty books were carefully studied and secretly introduced into my world of fantasy. In my own mind, I had created an exclusive club with a bizarre membership of people whom only I could summon to attend. The dreariness of my paid job was neutralized by my fascination with this anonymous society and the different qualifications I required of new members. The society remained active until I eventually changed my job. It was revived over the years whenever I was bored with what I was doing.

About this time I bought a twenty-year-old bicycle for 10/- and developed an expertise in freewheeling down the steep gradients of Buckinghamshire with my shoes resting on the handlebars. This irresponsible feat was eventually reported in the local newspaper where I was amusingly referred to as 'good circus material'.

'You're better known in my school than I am,' Maurice told me at that time. This fame was short-lived as Maurice excelled in his studies, led the Cadet Corps and eventually became head boy. His efforts to succeed academically absorbed all his leisure time and for a number of years our areas of common interest were largely reduced to matters that concerned the family. As a wage-earner I was beginning to identify more with my brother Sonnie and less with the younger members of the family. Unfortunately, the enormous demands made on Sonnie as the assistant Minister of the local Jewish Community limited the time we could spend together.

Weekends continued to attract family and friends to our home and Mother's incredible ability to improvise was reflected in the variety of home-made cakes and biscuits which always seemed available in large quantities

The constant flow of visitors created considerable interest and produced more than a few surprises. The large number of people who made a trek to our house overworked our doorbell and gave our lives a new dimension. Apart from a number of eminent scholars and teachers who frequently graced our table, the family developed close friendships with the local Chief of Police, Stanley Cox; our doctor, John Catherall; a retired clergyman, Henry Parsons, who were living in, or passing through, Chesham during the early part of the war.

Perhaps one of the most memorable visits occurred one very cold October morning. Maurice ran into the kitchen with an incredulous expression on his face.

'Mr Layman has come to see us.' He almost shouted the words.

We all rushed into the hall to welcome this old family visitor of our childhood. He was not just another caller. He was Mr Layman, the poor philosopher whom we had been taught to respect. The man who was rich in spirit and imagination and was only short on means. He was the man who had spoken of great thinkers as colleagues and nineteenth-century writers as fellow travellers. He had aged visibly. His old, black, Homburg hat looked quite grey from layers of ingrained dust. His worn brown coat hung loosely on his thin frame and his eyes appeared too large for his shrunken head. As we each shook his hand, we could see he was on the verge of tears.

'I only just heard of your loss,' he said, referring to Father's death, several months earlier, 'and I came to express my personal sympathies.' This poor, old man, in his late seventies, had saved pennies to accumulate the fare to pay his respects to us. When he removed his coat, it was quite apparent that he had lost a great deal of weight and we knew we were looking at a very sick man.

'How are you managing?' he asked my mother kindly. He spoke like an old friend rather than a respectable begger.

'I have good children,' she said, and immediately laid another place for him at our lunch table. For a long time he said very little, but picked sparingly at the food on his plate. He wiped his tongue over his lips a number of times and then suddenly we saw a tear roll slowly down his thin nose.

'I had a son,' he quietly announced, to our amazement. We

had never thought of his having a family or even distant relations.

'Late in life,' he explained, 'I had an unhappy, short marriage and produced a son.' We said nothing because there was nothing that any of us could think of to say. He caught the tear in his handkerchief before it dropped on to his plate and looked at each of us individually round the table.

'When David married out of the Faith, I disowned him,' he said, shaking his head and, as the second large tear began to follow the first, he sniffed, 'I was wrong. I should have known I was wrong.'

Sadly and slowly he told us that he had not heard of his son for many years until a telegram from the War Office informed him that he had died bravely on the beaches of Dunkirk. 'I deserted him,' he wept openly, 'and in the end he gave me as his next of kin.'

We looked down at the table waiting for Mr Layman to recover himself. 'With everybody else I took the role of a philosopher,' he continued in anguish, 'but with my only son, I had to play God.'

He wiped his eyes, attempted unsuccessfully to swallow a sob and then blew his nose. 'It is like a Festival being here with you all,' he said, cupping his face in his hands. Then, in a strange wistful tone, he added, 'Between birth and death, we can only try and enjoy the interval.'

This profound statement made a great impression on me, particularly as I thought it was typical of the old Mr Layman we had always known. It was not till many years later that I realized he was quoting the American poet, George Santayana.

He would not take any money from my mother when he left but he accepted a bag of food and fruit. We all felt we were saying good-bye to him for the last time and found it difficult to express our farewells in our usual voices. When Maurice and I saw this sad old man on to his train, he gave us both a big wink, 'I don't think I would have liked Voltaire,' were the last words we heard him speak. A great deal had happened since the first time we had heard him mention the philosopher and he spoke as if he were trying to bridge the years.

'I was shattered when he told us he had a son,' I confided to Maurice as we walked home.

'I don't think he missed him until he got the telegram,' Maurice said sadly. Some years later we learned that Mr Layman had died in an air-raid shelter and had been buried without any mourners.

It was fortunate that the office where I worked was within walking distance of my home. This enabled me to have lunch with the family instead of taking sandwiches each day. It was when I was returning to work, early one afternoon, that I was stopped by a Mr Becker. His problem was that his father-in-law, Mr Topol, had recently died, and additional help was required to perform the last rites. The ritual of paying the last respects to a dead person, by assisting in the washing of the corpse, was considered to be a good deed of the highest order. Although I willingly volunteered I found the ordeal a rather shattering experience. I had known the old man well and when he was, at last, laid in his coffin, I felt conscious that I had been recruited as an adult and not as a young teenager.

The actual funeral was due to take place in London so a few of us only followed the hearse to the corner of the road. As I turned away from the small procession I felt the arm of my Uncle Julius on my shoulder.

'There is no greater service you can perform for any human being,' he said quietly, but I was too moved to answer him. I had a strange feeling that I would have liked to have found a stranger and confided to him that I had helped a dead man into a coffin. It was an emotion I was to experience many times in the future when I passed another milestone in my life. On this occasion I knew I was going to keep my thoughts to myself as I had to get back to my job.

'Would you like to work in London?' my uncle asked suddenly.

Before I could answer he said, 'I have spoken to an important man in the diamond business and he has an opening for you.'

Two days later I met a Mr Prince of a firm called Henig & Company. He was the first millionaire that I had ever met and I was surprised that he smoked Gold Flake cigarettes and not cigars. He introduced me to a Mr Obstfeld, a Belgian Jew, who had a large diamond-polishing factory near Hatton Garden. I was taken on and employed at twice my previous salary, and immediately began to learn the trade under a Dutchman named Harry Beneen. He was a tall man with fair hair and he spoke very little. He swore that he would return to Holland to revenge the death of his parents as they had both been murdered in a concentration camp. Apart from making frequent mention of his intention, he dedicated several weeks to making me an apprentice diamond polisher. It was not his fault that he failed and it was decided that I was not cut out for the trade. Patiently, Mr Obstfeld spoke to me about his office problems and after questioning me for over an hour appointed me an assistant to his manager. This new position gave me an even higher wage and enabled me to cover a third of the family's overheads.

In order to arrive at the factory by eight, I had to get up at five-thirty and take the six-thirty train from Chesham to London. The working day finished at six and most evenings I attended classes in mathematics or English. On other evenings I continued my Hebrew studies with a Rabbi Dessler who was a great Talmudic scholar. He was an extremely humble and sympathetic man who was more than contented to believe that all the good deeds performed in this world would be appropriately rewarded in the next. I enjoyed studying with him although I could never share his dedication.

Soon after I began my office duties I was instructed to take the name of Harry Beneen off the list of employees. As far as anyone knew, he had simply stopped coming to the factory. In accordance with the regulations we advised the Labour Exchange and the Home Office and let the word get round Hatton Garden that we had a vacancy. Years later I learned that Harry had, somehow, found his way back to Holland and as the Germans had taken him for a Gentile, he was able to join the Dutch police force. He worked for British Intelligence until the end of the war and was directly responsible for the death of several Nazis.

Sitting in a restaurant in Amsterdam, wondering what to do with his future, now the war was behind him, his reverie was interrupted by a voice he had not heard for several years.

'We made it, Harry,' a man behind him said, placing his arm on his shoulder.

It was his brother, Jack, whom he had assumed had also been killed in the war. In fact Jack had spent the critical years on a remote chicken farm in Holland and had only come to Amsterdam, that very day, to buy a bicycle. They both emigrated to America where they built a large business importing a variety of French and Dutch cheeses.

While Sonnie and I were producing the income for the family, the younger members were all doing well at schools in Amersham and Chesham. During the Christmas holidays Maurice was able to make a financial contribution towards his keep by helping with the heavy work-load at the Post Office. We did not celebrate Christmas in any way but Mother did encourage us to visit the local hospital and take on jobs which enabled non-Jews to join their families for the festival. It was a practice which we both continued for many years in different parts of the world.

That particular year, the second Christmas of the war, we spent part of the day with patients who had no visitors at all. The wards of the Cottage Hospital were all decorated with ribbons and balloons and those who were sufficiently well sang carols and hymns with the nursing staff. A small contingent of young servicemen from a local RAF depot arrived with cakes and cigarettes and stayed to help clear up after the party.

I sat with an elderly local farmer named Tom Hollis and Maurice sat with a patient directly opposite. My brother said very little, but even at a young age he had the ability to appear sympathetic when he listened to others. Tom was a tough extrovert who considered his blasphemous tongue was a useful substitute for a college education.

'Oi tried to amputate me big toe meself,' he announced proudly. The announcement made me feel more sick than curious, but I managed to swallow hard and stay by the bedside.

'Do you have a family?' I asked as I could think of nothing else to say. The man laughed as though I had said something really amusing.

'Oi have that,' he chortled and, answering a question which had not yet been asked, he added, 'If I know me boys, they'll be too drunk to come and see me today and the old lady can't come alone.'

I listened to him boasting about the huge drinking capacity which he shared with his two sons and wondered why a toe operation should require the enormous dressing which covered his foot. Following my eyes, he said, 'I ain't going to pay for the whole cost of that bandage, I can tell you.'

When I left Tom Hollis, he gave me a cigarette and, very loudly offered his advice: 'You should start drinkin'. Put colour in your cheeks, it would.'

The remark seemed extremely funny to Maurice and me and we repeated it frequently during our two-mile walk home. It had been a very enjoyable day and quite unlike any festival which we observed in our own religion.

All the men at the factory brought sandwiches or rolls for lunch and ate them, together with downing a pint of milk which diamond workers were encouraged to drink. After I had been in the office for a few weeks I suggested to Mr Obstfeld that, as most of us took less than twenty minutes to eat, it might be appreciated if we finished work at five-thirty and reduced the lunch-break to half an hour. This suggestion was adopted and I was rewarded with an extra ten shillings a week. Spending the long working days in the strange atmosphere of a diamond factory gave me a great deal to tell Maurice each evening. Although our lives were now following distinctly different paths we were still able to share our thoughts and dreams with confidence and enthusiasm.

Occasionally, at weekends, we would join rambles and picnics and walk through the countryside between Chesham and Chorley Wood. At other times we would give free Hebrew lessons to the young sons of Jewish soldiers, preparing for their Barmitzvahs. This frequently took up several hours at weekends, but we considered the exercise a privilege rather than an obligation. It was about this time that I started smoking publicly, but at that stage Maurice was yet to find the habit enjoyable. Mother was not in favour of the practice as she believed, correctly, that it had contributed to Father's premature death. She would frequently discourage Sonnie and me but never actually forbade us to smoke. 'Bad habits in moderation can usually be controlled,' she once said, wisely.

Despite all the efforts which she made to cope with the household expenses, there was simply insufficient income even for the modest needs of a growing family. Without a great deal of discussion the lounge was converted into a bedroom for Maurice and me and our bedroom was taken over by an evacuee businessman who could afford to pay for his keep. He was a jovial, fat man named Moller who nurtured the belief that his large corporation made him attractive to the ladies. This idea was probably encouraged by the number of women who would turn and stare at his ungainly appearance in disbelief.

As a paying guest, Mr Moller was a kind, boring gentleman. He had built a comfortable business in London and spent his spare time indulging in a unique hobby which, to the best of our knowledge, he shared with nobody. He would borrow a large book, on any subject, from the library and make a 'guesstimate' of the total of all numbers mentioned in its pages. He would then start from the first page, making a note of every numerical figure mentioned and eventually add up the total. If this figure was within a thousand of his own, he would buy sweets for the younger members of the family. When the figures were far apart he would endeavour to explain, at great length, why he had lost his game. 'I'm really best with books on philosophy,' he would often tell us.

There was nothing nasty about the man but we children tended to treat him like a harmless idiot who helped to bridge a temporary financial gap. His obvious success in commerce enabled us to appreciate, at a relatively early age, that business acumen is not necessarily related to any intellectual ability.

One day when Maurice challenged him to a game of chess, he said, 'I could beat you, but I cannot stand playing a game where a queen has so much power.' It was this type of observation that prompted Maurice and me to think of questions for him in the hope that his often stupid answers would be quotable.

When Mr Moller left our house to live in a small hotel in High Wycombe, he told us that his current score in the game he had invented was sixteen – eleven against him. We were all amused by this piece of information as we knew that he had only borrowed a dozen books from the library altogether.

Our next guest was a Jewish lady of German origin. She was highly intelligent, but very dogmatic and when she discussed philosophy she spoke like a witness of the Revelation on Mount Sinai. We always believed that she would have been much happier if there had been proof that God had been born in Frankfurt, but she was a thoughtful if rather noisy soul.

During this early period in the war my sister Esther gave birth to her first child, Gerald. At this time too Sonnie was appointed a part-time Chaplain to the Forces. My youngest

Apprenticeship

sister, Judith had become a pillar of strength to her mother, although she was only just entering her teens. Apart from my job and my part-time studies, I was waiting impatiently for the girl across the road to drop her boy-friend. She never did. She married him.

XIX
Happy Birthday

My anxiety to play an active part in the war was initially frustrated by my being too young to participate. Each time Winston Churchill made a call to the nation to fight for freedom, I felt unfairly excluded from those privileged to respond. There was little one could do about it, but, in due course, I became old enough to join the Fire Service in a part-time capacity. The day I received the dark blue uniform was probably the most significant day of my life up to that time. At last I really felt identified with the war effort, although I didn't have much idea of the part I was going to play or the contribution I was to make. I enlisted as a trainee Despatch Rider because it sounded exciting and the training was relatively short. Furthermore, road map planning was the secondary subject and it was in this capacity that I had told my family that I had joined the Service. There seemed no point in worrying my mother unduly and I felt the white lie was more than justified. I simply had to remember not to wear the DR armband on my uniform when I was at home. For the first time I felt I had betrayed my special relationship with Maurice because I had not taken him into my confidence.

The training course took place at the rear of a disused railway siding in Buckinghamshire. The instructor, an amateur stunt rider named Bill, considered iron nerves and complete control were the main essentials for a man to qualify as a DR in twelve one-hour lessons. The final test required each student to jump off the pillion as the instructor rode past a sand-pit at about twenty miles an hour. When my turn came, I was alert and ready. As we passed the sand-pit, Bill shouted 'jump', and, with all the best intentions, I held on to him like grim death.

'Next time,' I yelled in his ear, and the next time round I was fully prepared, but at the last moment, I performed in exactly the same way. After five attempts, Bill threatened to fail me unless I jumped off the bike next time round. I still believe it was a miracle that I landed safely and did not kill myself. Three of us passed out of a class of six and we celebrated in a pub called The Three Tons with each of us buying Bill a beer. The last time I saw him was later that evening as he walked down Bath Road imitating a train.

Apart from cleaning my machine and delivering the odd parcel, I spent most of the next few months studying numerous routes to London from the surrounding counties. The purpose of this exercise was to be prepared to switch to an emergency route if bombs or fires made this essential.

The majority of the men on night duty smoked too much and were for ever drinking cups of tea. I cultivated both these bad habits which stayed with me till long after the war ended. Occasionally I was detailed to lead a fire trailer from our area to a major city in order to familiarize the driver with the route. Our actual fire drill was limited because, at that time, DRs were not permitted to join fire crews in any emergency.

The first time the chief Fire Officer of Southern Counties included our station in his call, German bombers had been raiding East London for several hours. Our senior DR had been taken ill and I was ordered to accompany a procession of some fifteen vehicles on a pre-arranged route to London. It was 2 a.m. and the night was pitch-black. The needle-thin ray of light thrown from our headlamps was certainly inadequate for the speed at which we were travelling. In less than an hour the crews were unwinding their hoses near the burning docks. The voices of hundreds of firemen, ambulancemen and air raid wardens were drowned by the aircraft overhead and the noise created by the fire itself. Shattered by the sheer horror of the spectacle, I sat astride my BSA motorcycle until I heard the voice of our duty officer.

'Report back to the station, DR. You have done your job.' I wanted to ask if I could help, but I knew I had to obey the order without question. I fired the engine and took the bike slowly round the fire engines and ambulances and away from the raging fires. Twenty minutes later I knew I was lost.

Completely preoccupied with the sight of London burning, I had forgotten to take the road leading through west London and had inadvertently travelled north. I was brought abruptly to a halt by a man in a dark uniform standing in the middle of the road. He was an officer in the Fire Service and I soon noticed numerous vehicles at all angles. He spoke with urgency in his voice. 'Are you on or off duty, DR?' he snapped.

'Returning to station, sir, I think I am off my route.'

'Leave your bike, you're back on duty.'

He handed me a large shovel as I got off the motorcycle. 'We've controlled the fires, but there could be two or three hundred people under the débris.' And then, staring through the darkness, he added, 'We are short of men, desperately short.' We had only moved a few yards when a man's voice brought us both to a halt. 'Can you help? I am caught.' The officer told me to stay with the man and left to find some help. The poor chap was buried up to his chest and there was little I could do alone. For a man locked into the fallen debris with a girder across his chest, my shovel was useless.

'Talk to me,' he said and I was aware of the tremor in his voice. I told him there was help coming and that I was a DR and that I had three brothers and two sisters and about my schooldays and how I wanted to enlist and my old English master. Suddenly I found I was sitting on the rubble and his head was resting against my arm and I was singing about the Isle of Capri

Happy Birthday

because he asked me to. A woman in uniform came along with a mug of tea and I realized I was thirsty and cold. I could not release my right arm very easily so I tried to wipe the rim of the mug with my free hand which must have been pretty grubby anyway, but it proved an impossible feat, and I knocked the mug over. I managed to light a cigarette which I offered to the man, but he said he could not smoke because he tasted blood in his mouth.

'Keep singing,' he said. 'I like old songs.'

I started singing the 'Isle of Capri' all over again and I then sang every song that came into my head. A doctor came along and gave the man an injection and said he would send help very shortly. I continued to sing and to talk long after I was conscious that it was a one-sided act. Eventually, in the thin light of dawn, I saw a rescue team approaching. I also saw that the man whose head was resting on my arm had his eyes and mouth wide open. I extracted my stiff arm from under his lifeless head and stood up.

'Sorry for him,' a team leader said. 'We have dug out over a hundred so far.'

I left them and, with a strange nausea racing through my inside, I rode back to the fire station. After reporting to the duty officer, I brushed my uniform so my mother would not ask too many questions and I rode home, leaving the bike several hundred yards from the house. I came through the door to find my mother making breakfast. She looked up and smiled. 'Happy birthday,' she said. I was seventeen.

When I reached my room, Maurice was waiting for me with an accusing expression on his face. 'You're a Despatch Rider, aren't you?' he said and handed me a letter from the fire service with the initials DR in front of my name. He had taken it from the postman to stop my mother finding it in the post. Before I could discuss the matter with him or apologize my head hit the pillow and I was dead to the world for several hours.

Three months later exactly I volunteered for the army and

was to see very little of Maurice or any member of my family for the following five years. When I left home Maurice was about to take his matriculation with his mind made up to follow a medical career. Apart from my shaving gear and a few family photographs, the only possession I took with me into the army in 1942 was a Hebrew prayer book given to me by my mother.